Happyslapped by a jellyfish

Happyslapped by a jellyfish

The words of Karl Pilkington

KARL PILKINGTON

DK Publishing

LONDON, NEW YORK,
MELBOURNE, MUNICH, AND DELHI
First American Edition, 2007

Published in the United States by
DK Publishing
375 Hudson Street
New York, New York 10014

Published in Great Britain by Dorling Kindersley Limited.
A catalog record for this book is available from the Library of Congress.

ISBN 978-0-7566-3635-7

DK books are available at special discounts when purchased in bulk for sales
promotions, premiums, fund-raising, or educational use. For details, contact:
DK Publishing Special Markets, 375 Hudson Street, New York, New York 10014
or SpecialSales@dk.com.

Color reproduction by GRB Editrice, UK
Printed and bound in by Butler & Tanner, UK

Discover more at
www.dk.com

All text and illustrations
by Karl Pilkington

Contents

Foreword

People always say "write about what you know". Well I don't know much, but I have been on quite a few holidays. Not cos I've wanted to, but because my girlfriend Suzanne likes it, so I always end up getting dragged along. She said it's cos she didn't go on holidays as a kid, which I think is a load of bollocks cos she didn't do much ironing when she was a kid either but she doesn't seem so eager to do that.

I've always said that if I won the lottery I would probably keep it a secret from Suzanne as I think it would end up splitting us up, as she would be forever booking holidays. The world isn't big enough to cope with the amount of holidays she'd want, and I'm not very good at visiting the same place twice cos you see everything you want to see the first time you go, which means the second trip is seeing the things you didn't want to see as much, which means it's not as good as your first trip.

I've stopped doing the lottery.

A few days at our mam & dad's

The following are extracts from my diary.

August 24th

It's a bank holiday weekend so we're seeing our mams and dads. We're at Suzanne's lot first. Her mam had bought me some Happy Face biscuits cos she knows I like 'em.

Her dad went out to play dominoes down at his local. We stayed in. Suzanne and her mam watched *Pretty Woman* with Julie Roberts and Richard Gere. It's rubbish. It's the one where Julie Roberts plays the part of a prozzie. She's nothing like a real one. She was playing chess at one point. I don't think real prostitutes would ever be playing chess.

I read me nature magazine. There was a moth that had

big wings. They were that big that the moth had to pack them away like a parachute after every flight. If I was that moth I would walk everywhere as I couldn't be doing with the messing about. It's the same reason I'd never buy a convertible car.

August 25th

Woke up with a sore throat due to the smoke from Suzanne's mam and dad's fags. Didn't sleep that well either as I had acid indigestion from the full packet of biscuits I'd eaten.

I went to get a paper from the shop. I saw three fat overweight cats on the way. No one looks after themselves that much up north, even pets. In London I think people go too far in the way they spoil their animals, but it's the other extreme up north. Lynne who lived three doors down from me had a cat that was that fat that it couldn't clean itself properly, cos it couldn't reach due to the fatness, so she used to vac it. It just lay there like one of them bear rugs that you see with the head still on 'em.

Stayed in all day cos the weather was grim. It was sleeting it down. The alarm on the chemist round the corner was going off for about two hours. I don't know why people bother having alarms cos no one takes a blind bit of notice. I can't be doing with noise. Noise pollution does me

SUZANNE'S MAM AND DAD'S PUB

Lots of smoke and strange folk
Regular laughing at his own jokes
Dog on a rope
Fruit machine broke
Old man in corner who never spoke

head in more than the sort of pollution that causes global warming. At least you can sleep through a snowstorm.

Had chippy for tea. After I've had chippy I always wish I hadn't. The idea of it is always nicer than actually having it.

Suzanne's mam had some fun size Milky Ways that she got off an old woman that she cleans for. I don't know why they are called fun size just cos they are small. If I said to a midget "Oh, you're fun sized", they'd kick off.

August 26th

Didn't sleep well again. I know why. It's cos I didn't do anything yesterday apart from sit and watch telly and eat.

I'm off to me mam and dad's today. I said I'll get them a laptop for their birthday. Their birthday was on May 11th but I said I'd get their present when I next saw them. Their birthdays are on the same day, so I only get them the one card between them. They say I'm tight cos I don't get them one each, but I don't see the point. I only get them one card between them for their anniversary so I don't see the difference.

The train was packed. We were on a table with a fat fella who worked in an IT department. He was harping on about how he's gonna run the company. He was fat and really unhealthy. He got up to get his lunch from the over-

head shelf and he got a sweat on. He also had some breathing problem – he snored even though he was awake. I had
to put up with it for three hours.

Me dad picked us up from the station and took us straight
to PC World to get the laptop I said I'd get. The fella in
there was trying to sell us loads of extras that we didn't
want. He was cross-eyed, which made it difficult to do a
deal with him cos eyes are important when doing a business
deal cos you sense trust through them, but I didn't know
which one to look at.

We got it back to their house and had a go at setting the
computer up for them. It wasn't easy. It took nearly four
hours. Me dad was getting annoyed and wished that we'd
just bought me mam a kitten to replace the one they had
put down a few months back. Me dad looked in the manual
and got even more annoyed with some of the instructions.
It said *click TCP/IP and choose either using PPP or manually
from the configure IPv4 as intrusted by your ISP. If you have static
IP type the address in the IP field.*

He has got no patience. I think that's where I get it from.
When I was a kid they bought me a ZX81 computer for
Christmas and I couldn't get it to work. It turned out that I
needed some extra memory for it and had to buy something
called a ram pack. Problem was, Tandy the computer shop

was shut and would be for about another week, due to it being Christmas. I was that frustrated that I was sick in the kitchen sink while me mam was peeling potatoes on the draining board.

Me and Suzanne went to bed. We decided to sleep top and tails due to the fact that me Dad had used his chainsaw on the mattress. He said it wouldn't fit in between the cupboards in the bedroom so he'd taken a few inches off. He then used heavy-duty staples and gaffer tape to seal where he'd cut. It's amazing how those few inches make such a difference.

August 27th

Woke up to the sound of me dad shouting at the computer. I could hear the noise it makes when you switch it on and off. I can't see 'em getting their heads round it.

I went down and showed me mam the sort of weird stories you can find out about on the internet. I found some news about some sheep that were chucking themselves off a cliff. Two thousand of them. It said how the first lot died, but as the pile got bigger the sheep started to survive, due to the fall being softened by all the wool.

Me dad said he hasn't got a computer to be reading about that sort of bollocks. Me mam then went on to read about a chicken that had four legs.

Me dad had got a dishwasher off one of his mates and I helped to fit it up. Me mam didn't really want one, but me dad said me mam shouldn't be wasting time washing up when they've got a machine that could do it. He then went on to say that while the machine is doing the washing, me mam can get on with the ironing.

We went into town and had a wander about. We left me mam to go off on her own as she doesn't like me dad tagging along cos she said all he ever says is "What do you need that for?"

We went and had a lolly and a walk about, looking in estate agent windows and that. We met me mam at the car an hour later. She had bought a colander. Me dad said, "What you bought that for? We've got two at home."

Me mam said, "Yeah but they've got holes in." I think she does it to wind him up.

When we got back the weather had cleared up a bit so me and Suzanne sat outside. I could hear the computer being switched on and off again. We were being bit by midges but Suzanne didn't want to go back in the house cos me dad would be mithering us about how the laptop works.

We are going home tomorrow.

SHEEP OFF A CLIFF

Thousands of sheep fed up,
So they jumped off cliff into bay.
They shouldn't survive,
But it just goes to show,
Where there's wool there's a way.

Wales

WHEN I WAS A KID we used to go to Wales for our holidays, and I loved it. We went to a campsite in Porthmadog. Me dad bought a caravan there – a nine berth, which meant it could sleep nine people. I don't know how they get away with advertising them like this. There were only two bedrooms, one with a double bed and one with two bunks, so to sleep the other five people meant pissing about with the Transformer-like furniture. If you had family staying, they would have to start getting ready for bed at about 8:30 due to all the messing about that was involved. The settee pulled out to sleep two, a cupboard door with strong hinges folded down and held one person, and then the table we ate at dropped down to make a bed. It was stupid. I'm surprised they didn't sell it as a ten berth and say you could use the oven as a cot for any kids or midgets in the family.

We went to the same site every year for about ten years, and we spent a total of about 10 weeks there each year. I should be able to speak Welsh, the amount of time I spent there. I tried to get me teacher to teach me Welsh instead of French cos I had no plans to go to France. He said I'll realise French is more useful when I'm older. I'm now 34 and I still don't agree with him.

I had loads of time off school to go to Wales for long weekends as well. My school had a real problem with kids having too much time off, so the teachers started handing out certificates for good attendance. If you did a full month without missing a day, they would give you a long weekend off. They gave a gold award for people who were never off, silver for people who were only off twice, and a bronze certificate if you were off for three days. I got a bronze. Once.

I had good times and bad times on the campsite. I was most happy in the arcade playing on the fruit machines. Me and a few mates used to go there every night at about 6:30 with £1 and stay till about 10:30. If I didn't win anything I'd hang around near old women who looked like they didn't know what they were doing, and when they looked stuck I'd help them win the jackpot on the off chance that they'd give me some of their winnings. It worked two out of three times.

I had a go on a fruit machine in a service station recently and was well confused. They're so complicated these days. When I was a kid, it was melons, cherries, plums, pears and grapes, which were the most expensive fruit and paid the jackpot. Now they've gone and added limes, peaches, some brown thing with green pips, and other stuff that I reckon Jamie Oliver would have trouble recognizing. I think there's less chance of winning on fruit machines now there's more fruit knocking about. I also noticed they've now added an automatic start so you don't even have to hit the start button. They take the fun out of everything these days.

If I wasn't in the arcade I would be on the beach. The beach was so big it even had its own rough area, where Hells Angels hung out on their motorbikes. Me Mam never wanted me to have a motorbike cos a lot of people on our estate died on them. She tried putting me off by saying "to become a member of the Hells Angels you have to poo in your pants and wear them for a week". Me dad said, "Your Auntie Nora could join today then".

The Hells Angels went up and down the beach at high speed, driving through jellyfish that had washed up on the

 sand. Did you know that a dead jellyfish can still sting you? I don't know why some insects have odd powers like that. Why are they still protecting themselves when they've been squashed to bits? All insects with special powers amaze me. There's even a frog with a poisonous back that has to get it's enemy to lick it. I'd like to witness how it does that.

I never went into the sea much cos there was too much seaweed. I didn't like the feel of it on me legs, plus seaweed is a good hiding place for crabs and other stuff. Me dad used to chuck it at me when I wasn't looking and wrap it round me legs. I couldn't swim, and me dad would always say, "When we go home I'm getting you swimming lessons". By the time we got home he'd forget about it, until they started showing adverts on the telly about learning to swim. Rolf Harris was in the adverts. I don't know why they picked him to do it, he's got nowt to do with swimming. It took me ages to realise it was him cos he didn't wear glasses in the water. I find it a bit odd when someone who wears glasses takes them off to clean them. They look naked.

There was another advert telling you to call the coast guard if you saw someone drowning, which also reminded me dad about swimming lessons. I don't know why this advert was on in Manchester. I used to try and turn the telly over before me dad realised what it was about, but that wasn't easy in the days before remote controls. Anyway, one day he saw it and decided to sort me lessons out.

I hated having swimming lessons. The main problem was that I was now 13 years old and all the other kids having lessons were about 8 or 9. I was at the age when hair starts springing out of all sorts of places on the body. I had more hair under me arms than the instructor. Some of the other kids thought I was the instructor.

I learnt to swim in about three weeks. The pool was rank. One day we watched another group of kids having advanced lessons while we were waiting. The instructor made them dive to the bottom, but rather picking up the usual rubber bricks, they had to collect old plasters and fag ends. I think it was a money-saving exercise as it saved having the pool cleaned professionally.

Me dad said, "now you've learnt, you'll be at the baths every week". Since then, I've been in a pool about eight times in 20 years.

People are always going on about global warming, saying how our summers are getting hotter, but I think they were hotter back then. I heard that, during one hot summer, some old woman on the campsite wrapped herself up in cooking foil to get a quicker tan. Problem was, she nodded off and cooked herself dead.

One year I caught chickenpox. I don't think there was any part of me body that didn't have spots on it. Me dad said I should go in the sea cos the salt would be good for the spots – that reminded him that he had to book swimming lessons when we got home. Me mam put some pink stuff on me face and I went to the arcade.

The arcade was run by a big Welsh woman called Cynthia, who gave you change for the machines. It wasn't long before she saw I had chickenpox and told me to leave, because of all the other kids in there. I was well fed up. On the way home I came up with a plan. I went straight to the wardrobe and got out me parka coat, which had a big hood with fur round it. I fastened it up right to the top and went back to the arcade. Then I got another regular kid to get me some 10 pences off Cynthia. I was just onto level two of Bubble

Trouble when Cynthia tapped me on the shoulder and asked me to leave and not come back until my skin had cleared up. I suppose I stood out in the crowd – everyone else had shorts and T-shirts, and there was me looking like Kenny from *South Park*. It took a week for the chickenpox to clear.

Me mam was glad I was banned cos it meant I'd be getting some fresh air instead. I had no one to play with cos all me mates were all in the arcade, so I ended up going on the beach with me mam. She loved it there. She used to collect loads of stuff like shells, dried seaweed and bits of washed up rope, and then she would put them in the caravan to make it feel more "holidayish". This did me dad's head in. When she wasn't looking he would chuck stuff out, so she started gluing it to mirrors and doors. She wanted a metal detector to use on the beach, but me dad said, "Bollocks to that. I don't want bits of metal shit stuck to the mirrors as well".

Me mam has always been into collecting stuff. When I was about six she'd take me and me brother to the local woods to dig up old bottles. We'd take them home and clean them and put them on the wicker bar that we had in the lounge. Me dad is used to it now. She can't go out without buying something useless to clog up the house with. Last time I went to see them, she'd bought a yellow plastic banana holder. The idea being that you unpeel a banana, bin the skin, and put the naked banana in the holder. Thing is, she doesn't even eat bananas, due to her having high potassium levels. She said she'll use it to put grapes in if she's going out, but I've never seen her use it.

I nearly died in Wales once. I was helping me dad and one of his mates collect slate from a big hill. Me dad wanted to stick it on the front of the caravan (he was getting as bad as me mam sticking stuff to the mirrors and doors), which he thought it would protect the caravan from bad weather in the winter months. We got to the top of this massive hill and found some decent-sized pieces. I was carrying one of them back downhill when the weight of it made me start to run. I couldn't stop. Me dad shouted out that I should throw meself on the floor, but I was travelling that fast, when I chucked meself on me arse I just bounced up and carried on running. I was hurtling towards a big slate wall at the bottom – if I ran into it I'd be dead. Luckily, me dad's mate was in front and had one opportunity to try and stop me. He dived and did a rugby tackle, grabbing me around the legs. I landed on me face and cut me head and scratched me cheeks.

Me dad gave me a bollocking for not being able to stop running. He does that when he's panicking. I was once choking to death on a Mr Freeze ice pop. Me face was red, me lips were purple, me eyes were rolling into the back of me head, and all I could hear was me dad shouting "that's what you get for being greedy". Me mam, however, opted to try and save me. She gave me one of them fireman squeezes and I got me breath back.

Anyway, we got back to the caravan and unloaded the slate, and then me mam went mad when she saw the state of me. There I was looking like Freddie Kruger. Because I'd been lifting the slate out of the car, me heart was pumping and blood was oozing out of the cuts. It looked a lot worse than it was, but I didn't mind cos she gave me a pound to cheer me up and off I went to the arcade. Cynthia couldn't chuck me out. I looked a mess but no one could catch anything off me.

Me mam and dad have now retired and moved from Manchester to Wales, so I still go there quite a lot. Last summer me and Suzanne went to see them, and me mam wanted to show us some local woods where she said there were six-foot witches and weird monsters hanging from the trees. Now, you're meant to pay to get in, but me dad reckoned that if you walk through three fields and climb over a couple of fences, you could get in the back way for free. He parked in the middle of nowhere and we started our walk. The first field was full of mud, we got stung by nettles in the second field, and the third one didn't seem too bad … until we got halfway across and Suzanne noticed a load of cows running towards us. She was terrified. She said she'd heard about people being killed by charging cows, so we all started to run. The cows were catching up with us. I didn't realise how quick a cow could run, but then again, why would I?

Suzanne was at the front, then me and me mam. But me dad had stopped and picked up a big log. He was standing with it, yelling as about 30 cows charged towards him.

They got about 5 foot away and came to a halt. Me dad then walked calmly to the fence and threw the log aside, like Russell Crowe in *Gladiator* after he killed that tiger. There we were, out of breath, covered in mud, and with our nettle stings even more irritated by the sweat from running.

Twenty minutes later we were walking round the woods looking at the witches and monsters. We were the only people there. We sat on a few tree trunks and ate some cheese butties me mam had packed (she didn't bring the grape holder), and drank a six-pack of orange juice cartons me dad got from Farmfoods – "they only cost £1 for six". He likes to tell everyone what he's paid for stuff when he thinks he's got a bargain.

We didn't hang around for long. Me dad wanted to go back the way we came but Suzanne was having none of it, so we ended up going out the proper front entrance. There was no one on the gate, so we probably wouldn't have had to pay anyway. It was when we went through the entrance that I noticed the prices – it would have only cost £1 each to get in. I asked me dad why we didn't just pay the entrance fee. "You could get 24 cartons of orange juice at Farmfoods for that", he said.

When I got home, Suzanne showed me loads of stories on the internet about people being killed by cows.

I LOVED THAT VEST.

THE HOT SUMMER OF 76.
THATS WHY IM JUST WEARING JUST
THE ONE JUMPER WITH T-SHIRT UNDERNEATH.

I'M THE ONE ON THE LEFT.

Ibiza

THIS IS THE FIRST PLACE I went abroad. I went with me mate Mark. He'd borrowed his boss's apartment for free, so all we had to sort out were the flights.

I borrowed one of me Mam and Dad's cases, which was far too big for what I was taking. I suppose this is why when I got to Ibiza airport I was stopped and asked to open my bag for inspection. I had nothing to worry about though, cos I'd packed it myself and knew there was nothing in it that would cause problems. So I thought. I opened it with the lid towards me while keeping my eye on the Spanish inspector. I noticed his eyebrows raise. I looked down and saw a garden gnome. It was one of me mam's. She loves garden gnomes and has them all over the house. She doesn't leave them outside as she says she feels guilty seeing their little cold faces when she closes the curtains at night. The one in my case was the one that usually sat by the fireplace.

I tried to explain all this to the Spanish man but none of it made sense to him. He just smashed it up to see if it contained anything – it didn't. Then he let me go. I called me mam to ask what she was playing at, and she said she put it there to look after me while I was away. I told her it had been smashed and she said, "That's OK, I've also put a gnome on a keyring in one of your socks." Here I was on my first holiday abroad and I've wasted the first 25 minutes of being on the island talking about gnomes.

I can't blame them for smashing it. Ibiza was known as a bit of a druggy party island back then. Most young travellers were probably carrying some sort of drug, apart from me. I went packed up like one of the *Ground Force* team.

I've never really taken drugs. I was put off by people on our local estate in Manchester who messed up their lives with them. I remember a girl in my history class who stood up halfway through the lesson and started screaming, saying she was being chased by a giant Mars Bar – she'd taken magic mushrooms at lunchtime. So I always avoided drugs, apart from the time I went to a music quiz at a local pub. On all the pub tables there were some little home-made

chocolates wrapped up in foil.
I love chocolate. I ate all the
ones on our table. After the
quiz I went round to the other
tables and asked people if they
were having their chocolates.
Most of them said no. I was
working my way through all
the chocolate like the fat Russian kid in Willy Wonka. It
wasn't till I got in a cab at the end of the night and couldn't
tell the driver where I wanted to go that I realised something wasn't right. The driver told me to get out. I was sat
on the kerb when a few people from the pub quiz came out
and told me I'd been stuffing me face with dope chocolate.
I didn't like not being in control of my body, so I've never
touched anything since.

We eventually got to Mark's boss's apartment. It was a
bit knackered-looking on the outside. Weeds had grown to
about three foot around the front door, and all the white
paint had bubbled in the heat and started flaking off. Still,
it was free and we'd only be using it as somewhere to sleep.
Mark found the key under an overgrown plant pot where
his boss had said it would be, and in we went.

I'd like to say the first thing that hit us was the stunning view from the balcony across the green hills of Ibiza island, but it wasn't. It was the smell of human shit. It was unbelievable. You couldn't escape it. Even if you held your breath, you felt like it was still entering your body through your pores. Me eyes were stinging from it. We opened the one window in the living room area and went into the bathroom to see if there was another window in there, so we could get a draught going to clear the air. That's where the problem was coming from. The toilet was half full of old poo. It couldn't be flushed away cos a hard crust had formed on top, like one of those caramel puddings where they burn the top with a welding torch. Still, what did we expect. It was free.

I emptied my case and then found that it was too big to put in any of the wardrobes, so I shoved it under the bed. This disturbed a nest of little green lizards. I don't know if green was their natural colour or just the effect of being locked up in a room smelling of shit for Christ knows how long. We'd pinned open the front door, and they all ran out gasping for fresh air.

We went for a walk to have a look around and to try and find a shop that sold bleach and a hammer to break the hard crust. The area seemed alright. Nice bars and places to eat. It wasn't easy finding a place that sold Domestos though.

One, cos most travellers don't need it, and two, the shop assistants weren't familiar with the brand and thought it was the name of a local restaurant. We found a Spanish version of strong bleach and headed back to tackle the blocked toilet. The smell hadn't gone. We poured the whole bottle in and left it to do its magic while we went for a drink in a bar.

One of my teeth started to ache. I've never had much luck with my teeth. I don't think my dentist was much good. When I was younger, he put fillings in all my back teeth, saying it would give them extra protection. He did the same with most kids. He'd look in your mouth and straightaway say his favourite line: "If there's a hole, it needs filling." Everything was done by knocking you out with gas back then, which left you feeling really sick and gave you a bad headache. People who don't suffer from tooth-ache never understand how bad the pain is – you can't think about anything other than the pain the tooth is causing you. The only time I've ever had worse pain was when I had kidney stones. The pain from them was that bad, I agreed to have a painkiller inserted up my arse in hospital by a gay nurse. I'm guessing his favourite saying was the same as the dentist's. Luckily, it didn't have to happen, as they found me an empty bed in A&E where they could inject me with morphine.

We went back to the shop where we'd got the bleach and bought some painkillers, but they didn't have any effect. I ended up having to get off my head with whisky so I couldn't feel the pain.

We got back to the apartment. The top layer in the toilet was floating a little, but underneath it seemed just as hard, so we decided to let the bleach continue its work through the night. I got into bed and saw a lizard on the ceiling. It was a big one. About the length of one of those Toblerones you can only get in airports. Normally I'd have to get something like that out of the room before I sleep, but I was that tired from the drink and the fumes from the bleach, I just nodded off.

In the morning the lizard had gone but the toothache was back. Mark was already up and ready for the first day of sun. His first words were, "Morning has broken but the second layer of shit in the toilet ain't." He looked a joke. He had Speedos on, a pair of shades and some flip-flops. He was that white, he was almost see-through like a jellyfish. I'm not happy walking round with next to nowt on, cos me body isn't that impressive to look at. I'm glad I wasn't around years ago when people had statues of themselves made, as you always had to be naked for them. Besides, it's never so hot that I can't handle wearing a T-shirt.

We went to the nearest bar so I could get some alcohol to numb the pain. Mark sat in the sun on a plastic chair with his legs apart, while I stayed in the shade with a whisky in me hand, watching *Only Fools and Horses* on the bar's TV. We used that bar every morning for my first few whiskies of the day. I ended up watching every episode of *Only Fools and Horses* and *Fawlty Towers*.

We didn't get up to much during the day – we just wandered about. I nearly got killed a few times in Ibiza by mopeds. All the people out there use 'em, no matter how old they are.

It's quite normal to see three people on a moped, and I once saw a farmer riding one with a goat stuck in a crate on the back. Nobody bothers wearing all the clobber that people in this country wear when they get on a motorbike. In Ibiza they believe that if you die, it was meant to be. On the corner of every street there's a bunch of fresh flowers marking someone's death patch. I think that's why the island looks so pretty. If it wasn't for all the flowers from all the deaths, Ibiza wouldn't be so green.

You can hire mopeds if you're on holiday, but I didn't bother cos me mam doesn't like me going on motorbikes. A fella on a motorbike once hit a lamppost at high speed on the main road outside our house. Me mam made the ambulance men a cup of tea, and they said his head was in good shape as he had worn a good helmet. The only problem was that the head wasn't attached to the body any more.

Mark was always looking at porn in the shops. They don't hide it in the shops abroad – it's just there, spread out for everyone to see. They even had rude stuff on the counter next to the KitKats. Every other shop, Mark would stop to see what rude mags they had in. It started to do me head in after a while.

It's getting a bit like that here now. I was buying a paper from Tesco's in Soho recently and they had *Gay Times* placed in the middle of *TV Quick* and *Chat* magazine. I've never really understood gay magazines. Why do gay fellas need pictures of nobs when they've got one of their own to look at?

In the last few days of the holiday I was getting a bit bored, so I said we should buy some cards as there's loads of good games you can play with them. Mark nipped out of the bar to get some and was back minutes later. "I've had me eyes on these for a few days", he said. He'd bought cards with rude photos on them – 52 pictures of filth. They looked like they'd been taken in the early 70s. I'd never seen so much body hair on a woman, and I still can't get the queen of spades out of me head. The fella on that one should have been a gymnast. Things weren't going too bad until a gust of wind blew the seven of diamonds off our table and onto the paella that the woman sat next to us was eating. She didn't look happy.

Mark wanted to go to a few of the clubs on the island, but I've never been into that scene. There were loads of them. He wanted to go to one that was the biggest club in the world, but I didn't see the point in that. The queue for the bar would be a nightmare. I'd prefer to go to the world's smallest bar. I keep seeing a lot about these big planes they are working on that can seat over 500 people. Again, not good. Imagine waiting to get your case off the carousel with all those people.

Anyway, we didn't have to go to the clubs to hear the music. We could hear it banging out at night when we were back in the apartment, as I nodded off after drinking 18 whiskies a day, and Mark fell asleep with the eight of clubs in his left hand.

The toilet was clear two days before we left.

WEIRD STORY THAT HAPPENED TO SOMEONE'S MATE THAT I KNOW

THIS WOMAN WENT ON HOLIDAY TO GET AWAY FROM HER HUSBAND WHO WAS DOIN HER HEAD IN. SHE WENT TO SPAIN SOMEWHERE AND WATCHED SOME OF THE LIVE ENTERTAINMENT THAT WAS HAPPENING IN THE HOTEL SHE WAS STAYING AT.

THERE WAS A LIVE HYPNOTIST ON STAGE MAKING A BLOKE THINK HE WAS A CHICKEN.

SHE COULDN'T BELIEVE WHAT SHE WAS SEEING AND DECIDED TO VIDEO IT.

SHE HAD A LOVELY WEEK AWAY AND WAS SOON BACK AT HOME WITH HER USELESS HUSBAND AND YOUNG DAUGHTER.

SHE POPPED ON THE TAPE TO SHOW EM WHAT SPAIN WAS LIKE.

THEY GOT TO THE PART IN THE TAPE WHERE SHE HAD BEEN RECORDING THE HYPNOTIST.

SHE WAS SO BUSY WATCHING IT THAT SHE DIDN'T NOTICE THAT HER USELESS HUSBAND WAS BEING TAKEN UNDER THE HYPNOTIST'S SPELL.

HE GOT UP OFF THE SOFA AND STARTED WALKING AROUND THE FRONT ROOM LIKE A BLOODY CHICKEN. SHE SAID, "IF YOU DON'T STOP MESSING ABOUT I'M GONNA STOP THE TAPE."

ANYWAY, HE DIDN'T STOP. HE CARRIED ON BEING A CHICKEN FOR TWO MORE DAYS. SHE STARTED TO WORRY ABOUT HIM AND CALLED HER DOCTOR TO GET SOME ADVICE.

HE SAID SHE SHOULD LET HIM WATCH THE REST OF THE RECORDING AS THE END OF THE HYPNOTIST'S ACT MIGHT SNAP HIM OUT OF IT.

BUT WHEN SHE PUT THE TAPE ON, SHE FOUND THAT SHE HADN'T RECORDED THE WHOLE OF THE HYPNOTIST'S SHOW, SO SHE COULDN'T USE IT TO SNAP HIM OUT OF IT!!! SHE COULDN'T THINK STRAIGHT DUE TO ALL OF HIS CLUCKING.

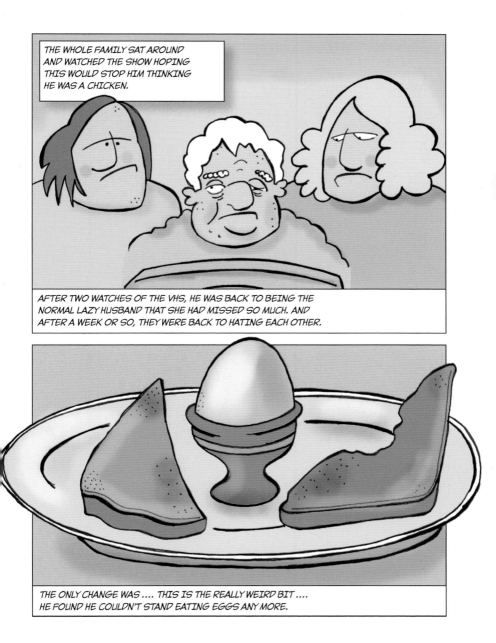

THE WHOLE FAMILY SAT AROUND AND WATCHED THE SHOW HOPING THIS WOULD STOP HIM THINKING HE WAS A CHICKEN.

AFTER TWO WATCHES OF THE VHS, HE WAS BACK TO BEING THE NORMAL LAZY HUSBAND THAT SHE HAD MISSED SO MUCH. AND AFTER A WEEK OR SO, THEY WERE BACK TO HATING EACH OTHER.

THE ONLY CHANGE WAS .... THIS IS THE REALLY WEIRD BIT .... HE FOUND HE COULDN'T STAND EATING EGGS ANY MORE.

Rye

The following are extracts from my diary.

April 28th

Going to Rye today for a few days with our mates Andy and Sarah. All I've been told about the place is that Spike Milligan lived there (Sarah is a big fan of Spike's) and the Battle of Hastings happened down the road.

When we got there we had some Battenberg cake. Sarah said Spike sometimes went days eating nothing but Battenberg cake. I hadn't had it before. I liked it.

We went and had a walk to find out where everything is. We found a few decent pubs, a chippy, and did the usual walk round a graveyard. We nipped into Budgens supermarket and got some more Battenberg cake.

Went to a really old pub that had signed pictures of celebrities on the walls. There was Chris Tarrant, Richard and Judy and some fella off *Bargain Hunt*. Had an early night cos I had a bad stomach from all the Battenberg cake.

April 29th

Didn't sleep very well due to an owl that was sat in a tree outside. I don't know why they stay awake all night if all they're gonna do is sit there tooting. They could do that in the day.

We went to the beach. We sat on the sand. I found a caterpillar. It was halfway between the dunes and the sea. I watched it for a bit. Like all caterpillars that I've watched, it didn't know which way to go, it kept changing directions. I don't see the point in them having all them legs and feet when they don't know where they are going. It probably couldn't see properly cos it was quite windy so it was probably getting sand in its eyes.

We went to a cafe that Sarah had said is in the top 50 guide of best cafes in the UK. I said it must be around number 48 cos if it was in the top 10 it would say so. Being in the top 50 isn't that impressive. I couldn't tell you what's at number 50 in the singles chart.

It wasn't that good. We ordered some sausage and egg butties and were given a battered old tennis ball on a stick with a number 4 on it (our order number). We sat at the back next to a really old, out of order *Space Invaders* machine. The butty was alright but I've had better.

There was a weird cat that hung around the cottage so we let it in. I'm sure the place was haunted. They say that cats, dogs and horses can see ghosts. Nothing was on the telly so I wrote in the guest book that we left the cottage a day early after we saw a ghost.

We are going to Spike Milligan's grave tomorrow.

April 30th

We got up early and set off to find Spike's grave. It was in a quiet little village. I'd heard that he has a message on his gravestone that says "I told you I was ill". We found it after about 20 minutes. Apart from his name it was all in another language, so we didn't know if it said "I told you I was ill".

We went into a little cafe. I couldn't understand how a cafe in a quiet place like this could survive. That was until we got the bill. £30 for a few sandwiches and a pot of tea. The fella who served us said that Spike used to go there. I bet it was his bill that killed him.

Sarah said it would be good to go and find where Spike used to live. I like Spike Milligan but I thought this was now getting out of hand. Three hours later, we were stood outside his old house. I was dehydrated after having to walk miles to get to it. It was in the middle of nowhere.

When we got back I sat and watched snooker with Andy. I had a right bad headache. Suzanne and Sarah made Sunday dinner. They turned the snooker off to watch *Chitty Chitty Bang Bang*. I said I've never understood why that fella opened a toy shop in a town where kids aren't allowed cos of the child catcher. Bad business. They told me to be quiet cos I was ruining it. I decided to go and buy some ice cream from Budgens. It was shut. That's the problem with little village type places. I stayed in Burnham Market recently and needed some milk but couldn't find any cos everything shuts on a Sunday by 4 p.m., except the posh hat shop. Everyone else had Battenberg cake. I didn't bother cos I was sick of it.

Los Angeles

OUR MATES Sarah and Andy were out in LA. Andy was working out there and had a flat, so they said we could stay with them for free if we sorted our own flights. I was looking forward to this trip cos I'd heard about the Ripley's museum they've got out there. It's a museum that has all sorts of weird stuff in it, like a man with seven eyes and people with small heads. I wanted to book tickets on-line for Ripley's but Suzanne said we wouldn't need to.

When we landed I was that knackered I felt sick. I couldn't wait to get some sleep. Unfortunately, before I could get into bed, we had to pump it up. The flat only had one bedroom, so Andy and Sarah had bought a blow-up bed to go in the lounge.

These beds should be given to homeless people as they come in a handy bag and are ideal to carry about. There are some homeless fellas who live on our street. I'm surprised they stay there cos it's a really noisy street. On some nights I've looked out of me bedroom window and noticed they've set up their bed and gone to sleep by quarter to ten. It's odd to think that homeless people sometimes have an early night.

They could also use inflatable beds in hospitals to sort out the bed shortage. Saying that, I think the shortage of beds in hospitals has now been put right, but that has created other problems. When I was in hospital last year with kidney stones they had enough beds, but the problem now is not enough pillows. That's the problem with problems, you sort one out and it makes another. I was rushed into hospital one night and ended up on a bed with no pillow. I reported it, and five minutes later the nurse turned up with one that was still warm as if it had just been removed from under someone's dead head.

Anyway, it was taking ages to blow up the mattress so we gave up when it was half full and just got on it. We didn't sleep that well. Each time one of us moved, the rush of air in the mattress pushed the other one out of bed. It was like trying to sleep on a bouncy castle. I was chucked off it at about 3 a.m. and landed on the remote for the stereo, which turned on the radio, which then started blasting out "Birdhouse in your Soul" by They Might be Giants. Every time I hear that song, I now think of that bloody pump-up bed.

The next day we went to the Ripley's museum. No one except me wanted to go. Suzanne was right, we didn't need to book – we were the only ones in there. I don't know why it isn't more popular.

Years ago, seeing odd people at the circus was a night out, but it doesn't happen so much now. I think Channel Five is responsible. A night doesn't go by without them showing a programme called *The Boy with an Arse Like a Chimp* or *The Girl with Arms for Legs*, so there's no need to see a live freak show. I've been interested in odd things ever since I went to school with two lads who had big heads and webbed hands. When I tell people about these lads, they think they were related. They weren't though. People think they'd have knocked about with each other as well. They didn't. I used to think their big heads and webbed heads were caused by a chemical plant near where we lived. There was another kid who had a pigeon chest. It looked worse than it was when he wore his school uniform cos his tie really stuck out. It exaggerated it. Then I saw the film *The Elephant Man*, which is probably the saddest film ever. It's about a fella called Joseph Merrick, whose body was deformed from big head to toe.

People gave him a hard time for not looking normal.

These days, when people are born with three arms or four legs, doctors try to whip 'em off. I wonder if we're interfering with nature too much. Maybe the human body is trying to evolve to cope with modern life. We now live in a world where we have to multitask, so what could be better than having three arms? The Elephant Man had a really big thick skull. Maybe this was nature's way of evolving us so we don't have to wear a helmet when we get on a bike. His brain would have had that much protection, he wouldn't have needed one. I look at some of these disabilities as superpowers.

Ripley's had some interesting things to see. In the first room they were showing short films. There was one about a dog that spoke and another about a bloke whose head was on backwards. He would have looked normal if he'd turned to look sideways. I like to imagine what it would be like to be in the position of someone like that. If my head was on backwards I think I'd learn to play the piano as pianists never face their audience, but he'd be able to.

It was quite dark and dusty inside with old pictures on the walls. There was one of the first Siamese twins playing chess with their doctor. That doesn't seem like a fair game to me. It didn't say who won.

The proper interesting stuff was kept in glass box-

es. There was a sheep with two heads, a kitten with two heads, and a five-legged cow. The weirdest thing was a man with six eyes. I wondered if he was unusually intelligent. I imagine he could have read more and taken in more information than most people, cos most of what we learn is taken in through the eyes. He probably never had to go on holiday to the same place twice cos he would have seen everything the first time. That was the only problem with Ripley's – they don't give you much information, so you had to use your imagination a bit.

We spent about two hours in there. I really enjoyed it. The others didn't.

The apartment block we were staying in had its own

pool. We got up early in the mornings so we could use it before the locals were awake, cos I wasn't comfortable walking about in swimming trunks in public. In LA everyone is really muscly and healthy looking. I think it's the weather that does it – when it's hot and sunny, you eat healthier food. I didn't have one Twix while I was out there. Instead I'd have a smoothie.

I had loads of fruit that I'd never had before in them smoothie drinks. I do like fruit, but I find that some of it involves too much messing about to get into. I mainly buy fruit that I can have as a snack when I'm out for the day. Apples are good for this. Bananas are good. Plums are fine. Pineapples are too much hassle. That's why you never see anyone buying pineapples in supermarkets. People should stop growing them.

There's too much fruit knocking about nowadays, and I think this is why we're told to eat five pieces a day – it's to get rid of it all. Once I was drinking some orange cordial and thought "this tastes a bit weird" and looked at the label. It wasn't just orange, they'd gone and slipped in some pineapple that they couldn't get rid of. This is happening more and more. I recently used some shower gel that had kiwi in it. That's another fruit no one wants. Oh and pomegranates, what a load of hassle they are. I once watched me mam eating one with a needle, one seed at a time, while watching *Dallas*. She only got through half of it. Like I said, we're not short of fruit, so why are we eating ones that are just made up of seeds. Stop growing 'em.

Anyway, I didn't actually do much swimming in the pool in LA, I just floated about in it. When the local fellas got in, I felt forced out. They wore trunks that showed everything off, and they started doing fancy stuff. I'm sure they were showing off in front of Suzanne and Sarah. They did the butterfly stroke, which I think is daft. It takes too much energy to do it, and why is a swimming stroke named after a creature that's rubbish in water? There's loads of fish they could have nicked a name from. Suzanne was enjoying watching the other blokes too much, so I said it was time to go. She said that was unfair cos they'd had to look at a load of rubbish at Ripley's to keep me happy. So I said I wanted to go back and stare at the model of a woman with four tits and see how she liked it.

We went to the beach and it was just as bad there. It was full of body-builders who were greased up to the eyeballs. It's not normal building up your body like that. It doesn't even look good, it's like a human version of *Pimp My Ride*. Who decided that it's good to have a six-pack? I think it's weird to see your insides through your skin. I don't like to be reminded that the body is crammed full of stuff, it makes me panic about how fragile I am. I do sometimes wonder if I'd look after my body more if I was better looking though.

We didn't go back to the beach.

We drove to San Francisco along Highway 1, a famous road that goes up the coast. We stopped off at a place called Carmel. It was a little village that didn't seem real – everything was perfect. They didn't have much there, just a few hat shops and a couple of shops that sold cakes for dogs. I went on the small beach. They had squirrels running about. People were feeding 'em all sorts of posh food. It annoys me a bit how people like squirrels but not rats. At the end of the day they're the same thing, except that squirrels have had a better upbringing.

I've noticed a big change in the squirrels in our local park. They're getting really fat cos people keep feeding them Mars bars and biscuits, and all the sugar they eat is making them more aggressive. If you give them an acorn, they now turn their nose up at it. Every type of creature is changing its diet. I once caught some sort of little grub-type insect on my windowsill that was carrying off bits of the digestive biscuit I'd been eating. It's weird how me and that insect are miles apart in terms of lifestyle, yet we both like a biscuit.

We used the car's sat nav to get to San Francisco. I think

sat navs have taken the fun out of travelling. I like getting lost, cos that's how you find new places – I've found loads of new cafes in London just by wandering down the wrong street. Columbus would never have found America if he'd had a sat nav fitted on his boat.

Suzanne had booked a basement flat in San Francisco. It was basic and smelt a bit musty but was OK. The owner lived upstairs with her 40-year-old son, who was a bit odd. He stood outside in the garden looking at us through the window all the time. This was quite a good thing in a way, cos he made us want to get out of the flat, which meant we saw a lot of stuff while we were in San Francisco.

We did a trip round Alcatraz Island, which used to be a prison. It turned out to be the best tourist thing I've ever been on. They give you a little iPod-type thing with headphones to listen to as you walk. There were interesting stories told by past inmates and facts about how people had tried to escape. It was nothing like the school trip I once went on to Styal women's prison in Cheshire. All we saw there was a five-a-side netball game played by women with tattoos, two of which were shouting "fuck off you shits" at us as we walked around the perimeter fence. Our teacher Mrs Turner pretended it wasn't happening. I still don't know why they took us there.

When the boat took us back to town, I noticed that San Francisco had a Ripley's museum as well. Before I even had chance to say "can we go in", Suzanne said "NO". She said that once you've seen one two-headed sheep, you've seen them all.

San Francisco is good. The only sad bit is that it seems to have a lot of homeless people who are legless. When I say legless, I don't mean off their head on drink – I mean they didn't have any legs. They got around on skateboards, which made me wonder why they decided to live in San Francisco, cos it's not ideal for them. Not with all those hilly streets about. One night we were in the flat watching telly, trying to ignore Brian looking through the window, when we saw our street on the news – one of the legless homeless had been shot by a policeman. The copper was saying how he thought the homeless fella had a shotgun. Turned out it was just a false leg. We decided to stay in that night and have a pizza.

The next day we went on a bus tour around San Francisco. The driver was a bit annoying. He kept cracking jokes that you could tell he does with every bus-load of people. He was very pale with ginger hair, and he must have been quite proud of being ginger cos he also had a big ginger moustache. In England people seem to get quite a bit of stick for being ginger. Even ginger cats look fed up and are normally fatter than other cats, probably because they turn to food for comfort.

The bus driver took us to see an earthquake-proof building, which isn't that exciting on a day without an earthquake. Then he took us to see where they filmed the kids' TV series *Party of Five*. Suzanne and Sarah remembered the programme. I didn't. He said be careful if you get off the bus to take photos of the houses from *Party of Five* as there's a lot of dog shit in the grass, and he didn't want us walking it onto his bus. He didn't stop talking for the whole tour. I remember thinking how much he sounded like Shaggy out of *Scooby Doo*.

He then pointed out where the gay area was. He said he didn't want to take us there cos it wasn't a very desirable or nice area. Which I thought was odd seeing as he'd just given us 10 minutes on dog-shit hill. He also said, "there are quite a few prostitutes in San Francisco and some of them are laaaadeeeboys, so you have to be careful cos you never know what you might be geeeeetttttin" – and then laughed to himself. At least he was enjoying it.

I liked me time in LA and San Francisco.

I have since found out that there's a Ripley's in Blackpool.

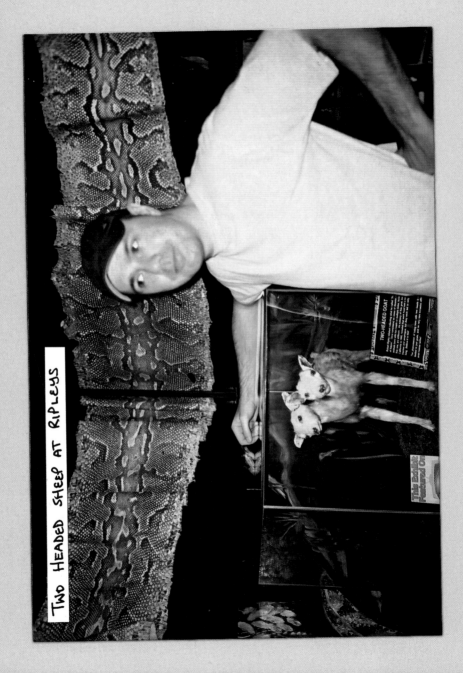

TWO HEADED SHEEP AT RIPLEYS

DOG SHIT SQUARE IN SAN FRANCISCO

COCKY SQUIRRELS IN CARMEL

LAZY SEALS

ALMOST EVERYONE HAD SEEN HER IN SOUTH AFRICA SO SHE TOOK A PUNT AND MADE HER WAY OVER TO ENGLAND. I DON'T KNOW HOW MANY SEATS SHE USED UP.

BEFORE SHE KNEW IT, CROWDS WERE FLOCKING FROM EVERYWHERE TO SEE HER AS THERE WEREN'T MANY OTHER ATTRACTIONS. REMEMBER, THIS WAS YEARS AGO WHEN MADAME TUSSAUDS AND THE LONDON EYE WEREN'T EVEN IDEAS ON PAPER.

SHE WAS POPULAR IN ENGLAND BUT SOON DIED AND WAS SENT BACK TO SOUTH AFRICA TO BE BURIED.

I DON'T KNOW IF SHE'D BE HAPPIER LIVING TODAY AS THOSE SORTS OF SHOWS WOULD BE FROWNED UPON. SO I DON'T KNOW WHAT SHE WOULD HAVE DONE FOR A LIVING.

BUT I TELL YOU ALL THIS COS IT REMINDS ME OF ANOTHER STORY OF A WOMAN WHO WAS FAT. SHE DIDN'T HAVE THAT ILLNESS. SHE WAS JUST PRETTY FAT. SHE WAS GETTING DRESSED ONE MORNING AND NOTICED SOMETHING ODD ON HER ARSE CHEEK.

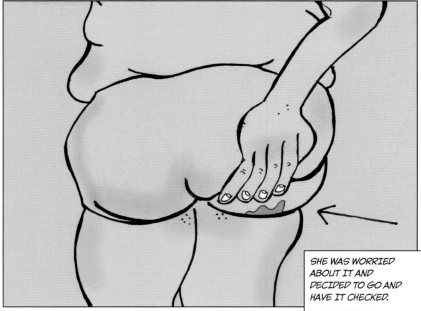

SHE WAS WORRIED ABOUT IT AND DECIDED TO GO AND HAVE IT CHECKED.

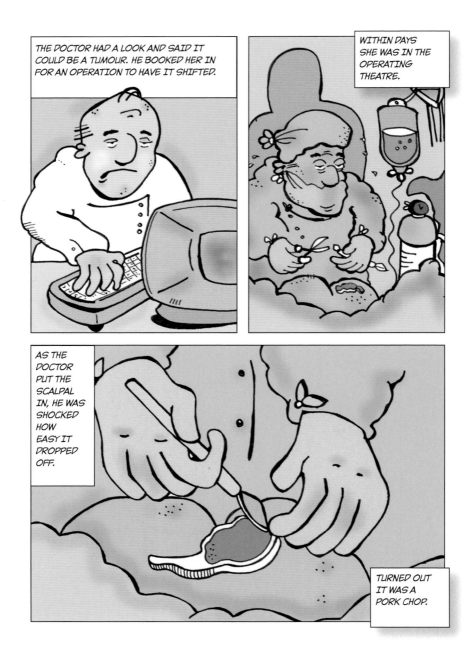

WHEN SHE WOKE, THE DOCTOR SAID IT WAS A FALSE ALARM AND THAT IT WAS IN FACT A PORK CHOP THAT WAS STUCK ON HER ARSE.

SHE REMEMBERED EATING HER TEA ONCE AND THINKING HOW SHE COULDN'T REMEMBER EATING THE CHOP, EVEN THOUGH IT WASN'T ON HER PLATE. IT MUST HAVE SLIPPED OFF AND ENDED UP ON THE SOFA.

BEFORE THEY SENT HER HOME, THEY SERVED HER PORK CHOPS AND CHIPS.

HA HA

THAT LAST BIT IS MADE UP, BUT THAT'S WHAT THEY SHOULD HAVE DONE.

Tenerife

THE FIRST TIME I realised Suzanne liked to be treated like a proper lady was when we moved in together. I'd bought a new bed, but when it turned up there was no mattress. It turned out that you had to buy the mattress separately, which is stupid. A bed without a mattress isn't a bed. It's a climbing frame. Anyway, money was a bit tight, but me dad said that uncle Alf had a spare mattress that he'd bring round. Alf wasn't a real uncle, he was just me dad's mate. I don't know why he was sold to me as an uncle.

Me dad dropped off the mattress and I made the bed. Suzanne came in from work a few hours later and the first thing she said was, "what the hell is that smell?" She traced it to the mattress, which stank of diesel cos uncle Alf had kept it in the back of his van. In the end I had to buy a brand new mattress. It took two days for the smell of diesel to shift.

So, cos of the mattress incident, I knew within minutes of walking into our hotel room in Tenerife that Suzanne wouldn't like it.

The beds and pillow cases were stained, the air con didn't work, cockroaches were running about on the sideboard, and we didn't have our own bathroom – which I wasn't happy with, to be honest. If there's one thing I don't like, it's feeling I'm being rushed when I'm on the toilet. Every time I was sat on the hotel loo, I would hear someone outside waiting for me to finish. It was pointless taking in a newspaper cos I never felt I had time for a proper read. Maybe I should have picked somewhere better for our third anniversary together.

We had a balcony that overlooked another hotel. I sat there many a day listening to the young girls next door shouting to the lads in the hotel across the way. The only time I couldn't hear the girls talking was when Ronny was playing the organ downstairs. Ronny worked in the hotel bar and played all the classics, like "Sweet Caroline" and "I Just Called to Say I love You". He had jet-black hair that I'm sure was a wig. It's the back of a wig that always gives it away, and seeing as he was usually sat at the organ, that was the bit you saw the most.

I'm good at spotting a wig. When I first went round to Suzanne's mam and dad's, I nipped out to the off-licence to get myself a Walnut Whip and spotted that the fella who runs the place wore a wig. I got back and said how bad it was, but they said, "what you talking about, he doesn't wear a wig!" They didn't believe me until they'd been to the pub and had it confirmed by one of their mates. He's run the off-licence for years and they'd never noticed.

Maybe I take more notice of hair cos I haven't got much. I started going bald when I was about 23. I think it was caused by once having to work a 24-hour shift at a place where I used to pack cassettes. It was my job to shrink-wrap them in cling film. We had a big rush-job on because the comedian Chubby Brown had released a rude version of the song "Living Next Door to Alice" with the band Smok- ie, and it had done unexpectedly well in the charts. I had to shrink-wrap 10,000 copies so they could go out to the shops as soon as possible, and that meant working through the day and night. A couple of days later, I noticed a bit of baldness on me head.

Me mam says it's got nowt to do with it. She says I went bald either because I once mistook her blonde hair dye for shampoo or because of the rubbish hairdresser's me dad used to take me to. It was in a little shed next to a train station. The barber had to pause every time a train passed to avoid taking your eye out with the scissors. His busiest time was the last week of the summer holidays, when all the kids got their hair cut before going back to school. If you called for an appointment he'd book you in according to the train timetable. He'd say, "I can fit you in between the 16:35 and 16:56 trains to Altrincham."

Me mam thinks I picked up some head disease from the sink he used to wash my hair in, cos he would also use it to pop his dirty cups with fag ends in. I stopped going there and went to another place that wasn't much better. It would take ages to get a haircut cos they were forever trying to flog you knocked-off gear. You'd go in for a haircut and leave with a packet of five blank VHS tapes and a pirate copy of *Now That's What I Call Music! Vol 2*.

Even though I was quite young when me hair started falling out, I never thought of getting a wig. If I was to wear a wig, I wouldn't stick with one style – I'd change it every day. Have different colours and that. If you're gonna wear a wig, make the most of it, but don't think you're conning people into thinking you have hair. If being bald really bothered me, I'd rather wear a hat all the time than a wig.

Anyway, Ronny the organ player definitely had a wig. He also had a pale, gaunt face and a white suit that was too big for him. He played his organ non-stop from about 5:30 until 11 p.m. The only time I saw him stop was when some drunk woman went and stood by him and started singing along to "We'll Meet Again". When he finished the song the woman wanted to sing another, but he was having none of it. He got up and went to the bar. He had one drink and then went back to his organ and played an instrumental track, "Stranger on the Shore" by Acker Bilk, so the woman couldn't sing along. She looked well put out.

Whenever you left the hotel you got hassled by people flogging stuff like packs of perfume and handbags that were replicas of expensive makes. Fellas would give you scratch-cards and tell you to scratch off the silver bits straightaway in case you won something. You'd scratch it off and they'd say, "Look you got three suns – you've won! Come with me to the office and pick up your prize." I'd say go and get it for me while I wait. It was a load of bollocks – they just wanted to get you into their boss's office to sell you time-share. I told one of them I was under 18, cos they weren't allowed to offer timeshare to minors, and the cheeky bastard said "You're under 18??? You must have had a tough paper-round then!" I wanted to say "No, it was shrink-wrapping 10,000 cassettes for Chubby Brown that made me look this old you cheeky get."

On our anniversary night we had our tea at one of the English bars and then went for a wander about. We heard the voices of the girls from the room next door. I hadn't seen any of them yet due to the concrete wall between the balconies. It's weird how what you imagine can sometimes be so accurate – their arms were as wide as their legs, and they looked like they had no top teeth. All of 'em wore white with high heels to match. Two of the lads from the hotel across the road were with them. They were queuing up to go on this ride where you get locked into a round metal frame and then fired about 150 feet into the air. I'd seen sturdier stuff made with Meccano. We watched that for a bit and then went back to the hotel.

I went into the toilet that was unlocked. There were five women inside and a young lad asleep on the bath mat. I said I wanted to use the toilet. The women said they'd go but would have to leave the young lad asleep as he hadn't been well. They said something about how they'd been waiting three hours for their room to be ready. I didn't bother using the toilet as I wouldn't be able to relax with a kid asleep on the floor. I'm like a cat when it comes to using the toilet – I don't like being watched. It's pretty rare to see a cat pooing. They never do it if there are people about. Dogs yes, cats no. When we had kittens at home, if I ever went to watch one of them use the litter tray they would always turn their back to me. That's what I'm like.

Anyway, it was our anniversary night and I thought I'd treat Suzanne to a bit of the other. It was weird having it away to the sound of Ronny's organ. I kept trying to work out what each song was from the first few notes, like they used to do on *Name that Tune* with Lionel Blair. I was happy doing that when we were disturbed by a loud banging at the door. I thought it was the girls from next door messing about, so we ignored it and carried on with the business. But the banging continued and then we heard a man's voice saying "is there anyone in there?" I got out of bed and answered the door whilst hiding me tackle. Stood there were three firemen. One of them told me to get out NOW cos there was a fire. Suzanne heard what was said and was up and dressed in seconds. She doesn't cope with danger very well.

It was chaos outside. Some people were crying, some were shouting. Someone was walking round asking people to get together and sue the hotel, and bar staff were handing out free spirits to calm people's nerves. The five women I'd bumped into in the toilet were already outside and the kid was awake. Everybody was outside. This would have been the best time in the whole holiday for me to use the toilet.

It turned out to be a fire in a wheelie bin that had set light to the door of one of the lower rooms. Luckily, our room was OK, which was a relief to me as I'd spent me last few quid on a replica Gucci handbag for Suzanne's anniversary present.

Florida

WE DID THIS TRIP even though we couldn't really afford it, and Florida isn't really my kind of thing as I don't like fairground rides. I've never understood why they always send sick kids to Florida. Going on all them rides is only going make them feel worse.

When I was at school, kids looked forward to day trips to Alton Towers, which is like England's version of Disneyland, but I didn't bother going. I was happier going into school that day, as hardly anybody else was knocking about. There was normally a placement teacher who looked after a few of us, and they would let us just sit and draw. The next day, all the kids who went to Alton Towers would have to write about it, which meant I had another day of drawing.

The only daytrips I went on while I was at school were a tour of Kellogg's, an afternoon at a women's prison, and a trip round *Manchester Evening News*, where I caused a load of hassle cos I left early without telling anyone – I had a job at Cordon Bleu supermarket to get to. Mr Carpenter gave me a bollocking the next day cos he thought I'd been dragged into one of the printing presses. Still, the bollocking wasn't as bad as the one I would've got from me boss Paul at Cordon Bleu. He was a right knobhead. Your work was never good enough for him. In the end he sacked me for whizzing through a big puddle out the back in a Cordon Bleu shopping trolley. He found out cos the trolley got caught in the blocked grid in the middle of the puddle. Me mate passed me two long ice pops that I used to stab at the grid to try and unblock it, but then Paul came out to sign for a delivery of Pot Noodles and saw me. He sacked me on the spot. He didn't even wait for me to get out the puddle. When I went in on the Friday to pick up the money they owed me, he'd taken out £1.20 for the two ice pops. I hated me time there. I only worked there cos Tesco wouldn't have me.

Anyway, Florida. Suzanne's brother came with us on this holiday, so he went on the rides with Suzanne while I stood and watched. I only went on two. The first one went really slow and played the nursery rhyme "It's a Small

World" over and over again while you passed weird-looking dolls from all over the world. Adults didn't seem to go on it – they just sat their young kids on it and waved them off. Everyone was smiling and waving at me. I think they all thought I was a bit mental.

The other ride I went on was "Living with the Land", where you float on some sort of raft and go past green houses, plants and veg. No one was really interested in this ride. It was just me and three old women who were like the *Golden Girls*. They were going on about the size of a massive eggplant that we passed. I had no idea if it was big or not cos I'd never seen an eggplant before. I think there is too much stuff in the world, and proof of this is when things share the same name. An eggplant has no link to the egg we eat. I was in a fish shop a few weeks back and they had something called a "cow fish". It didn't even look that much like a cow, it just had a bit of a flat face and a pair of horns, which isn't enough to be named after a cow for me. We're running out of words.

I was on this raft looking at an eggplant with three old women who were panicking cos they were all trying to get a picture of themselves with it before the raft moved on to the big marrow. Everything is massive in Orlando. The problem is though, cos everything is so big, nothing looks big, if you get me. People always have a go at Americans, saying they are too big and fat, but I put it down to the fact that Americans make everything so big that they don't realise how big they've got themselves, until they visit a small village in somewhere like England where they can't fit into a normal-sized shop.

We were staying in a motel while we were in Florida. It overlooked a car park and a busy road and was next door to a Denny's. Denny's is an American-type diner whose gimmick was selling square burgers with the catchphrase "We don't cut corners at Denny's."

I thought I was gonna die in that motel room. It all started when we'd been out all day in one of the parks. We were waiting for the bus to pick us up when the sky went from being blue and clear to black. The park seemed to empty pretty quick, so there was just me, Suzanne and her brother left standing in the middle of this big car park. It started to chuck it down like I've never seen before. And then the lightning started.

I've always been a bit worried about lightning ever since I read that there was a woman who was in her house brushing her teeth when lightning hit her roof, passed through to the tap she was using and then jumped from the tap into her mouth, went through her body and left through her arse.

That's why I don't like lightning. It's unpredictable. The only place we could shelter was at a picnic table that had a metal roof on it. I sat there with my mouth shut.

After a 30 minute wait, the bus turned up. Suzanne told the driver where we wanted to go and paid, while me and her brother went and found some seats. The driver took us right up to our motel entrance, which was nice of him as the bus stop was quite a walk from the motel. All the other people on the bus were bickering cos it had gone off its route, but I just thought he would be doing the same for most of his passengers with the weather being so bad. It wasn't until we got in our room and counted our money that we found out why he'd been so keen to drop us off at the front door – Suzanne had tipped him about £40. It was at this point we realised that none of us had brought any type of bank card and we only had about £70 between the three of us. And we still had three days in New York to come. We were sat there counting up our change to see if we had enough for a takeaway pizza when there was a weather alert on the telly saying how there are bad storms over Florida with a chance of tornadoes.

We were looking in the motel draws to see if there was some kind of leaflet telling us what to do if a twister is in the area when the motel was hit by lightning. There was a big crack and then an alarm went off. Alarms stress me out. I don't understand why alarms have to make a horrible noise. If I had an accident and was in the back of an ambulance whilst I was all wired up to oxygen and stuff, the noise of the siren would stress me out and make me feel worse. It must be the same for doctors when they do operations. I've seen it on *Casualty* – someone's heart stops and the machine does that long tone. If I was a doctor I'd work better if the machine played a happy tune when everything was going OK and some sad, calming song if the patient was dying. I discussed this with me mates once, about how as long as the noise is recognised as a warning sound, it could be anything. It could be the sound of a chicken or a duck. It wouldn't be as bad on the ears as the usual siren and yet everyone would still get out of the way. Me mates said it was a stupid idea and that the sound of a loud chicken would be worse. It's all subjective innit.

We found a leaflet in the motel binder stuffed in next to a Denny's takeaway menu. It had details of what to do during a tornado, lightning storm and earthquake. It was the same rules for all three. It said we should stay indoors, and if a twister got close, we should get in the bath and place the mattress on top. I started to laugh cos this is how I deal with fear. Here we were about to be whisked away by a giant twister, and we'd be in the eye of it, sat in a bath like a scene out of *Last of the Summer Wine.*

We stayed in watching the telly for updates on the tornado situation, but after about two hours the rain calmed down and the lightning stopped. We decided to go out for food and celebrate the fact that we were still alive.

We ended up in a steakhouse. It was like the Aberdeen Angus Steakhouses we have in London. You read the menu and it all looks fairly reasonably priced, but then when you get the bill, it's three times the amount you expected and you realise they have charged you per chip.

We paid the bill and left a small tip cos we were now really short on cash. As we were leaving through the front door the waiter shouted at us. I thought we'd left something behind. It turned out we hadn't given a big enough tip, and he shoved what we had left into Suzanne's hand. I didn't mind as we needed every penny possible to get us through our three days in New York.

New York

WE HAD TO CIRCLE New York for 40 minutes before we could land. I could hear people saying the view was amazing, but we didn't really get to see it cos we had our heads in sick bags, cos we'd eaten loads of packets of free nuts to fill us up, seeing as we had no money left for food after spending it all in Florida.

I don't like flying. It doesn't seem normal to be whizzing along at high speed 30,000 feet up in the air. The other thing I find odd is how airlines seem to take on pilots on the sound of their voice and not their flying skills. Why is it you never get a northern fella coming on the mic saying "alright ... it's ya captain 'ere ... how's it going?" It's always a well-spoken posh fella.

The airport was well busy. We were met by a fella called Ernie, who looked like the druggie played by Sean Penn in *Carlito's Way*. If you haven't seen it, Ernie had big curly hair, big glasses and an old purple suit. He was friendly in that New York kind of way, where being friendly is just acknowledging that you are there. "Welcome to the Big Apple", he said. I don't know what it is with America and big fruit. Massive eggplants in Florida, now big apples.

He seemed eager to get us out of there. We thought it was because he wanted us to have a good time in New York and not waste any more time at the airport, but it wasn't that. It was because he'd parked right outside the entrance in a no-parking area. A traffic warden was putting a ticket on his big old car. He went mad. He was effing and blinding and calling the warden a "mutha fukka" whilst opening the car doors for us and saying "I hope you enjoy your stay".

The weather was roasting and his car had no air con. The traffic was hardly moving. Ernie said he'll take us a better route to the hotel. I thought he meant a better tourist route so we could see some of the sights. I was wrong, he meant a short cut. We passed gangs stood on street corners, prostitutes, drag queens and homeless people. Just as I thought he was gonna do us over and take our last £70, which we had to make last for three days, he turned right and there was our hotel.

It was just as busy and noisy in the hotel reception as it was at the airport. They say New York is the city that never sleeps. I'm not surprised with all the racket. After a load of faffing about we were shown our room, which was basic but clean. They'd put up a camp bed for Suzanne's brother and there was one small window that overlooked a load of air con units, but you couldn't hear them due to all the police sirens.

We decided to go for a wander. The front door of the hotel hadn't even fully closed when we heard a scream – a woman had been mugged and her handbag had been nicked. I got a quick glimpse of the robber's face but I didn't want to get involved. If the woman had been attacked, maybe I would have done, but I'd been put off getting involved in crime a few weeks before.

At that time we were living on the tenth floor of a tower block in Salford. There was always trouble round there. I once nipped down the road to the Happy Shopper supermarket and the flat above was on fire, with flames gushing out of the smashed windows. People were still going in and out of the shop, so I popped in to get some milk. A fireman was having an argument with the fella who ran the place and telling him to close the shop until the fire had been sorted, but the owner was saying, "it's bloody peak time this".

If nothing was on the telly I used to sit by the window in the flat and watch explosions on the field as joyriders blew up the cars they'd nicked. One evening when Suzanne was out, I saw two lads smash the window of a neighbour's car. They released the handbrake and started pushing it down the road. I called the police, reported it, and then went to bed, cos I was working nights at the time and wanted to get a few hours kip before I had to go.

I was just nodding off when the phone went. It was the police: "Can you tell us where they pushed the car to?"

"I think they were heading for the main road but I dunno." The police knew I was in a block of flats and asked me to have a look. I said how I was tired and needed to get some sleep before I went to work, and hung up. They called back and said they were sending a helicopter over and wanted me to point to where the lads had headed. There I was, ten stories up, knackered, stood on the balcony in me undies as a helicopter put it's beam on me. I pointed them off to the roundabout, went back inside, and took the phone off the hook.

Anyway, we had a wander about New York without spending any money – for three whole days. We went into museums and looked at Chinese, African and Indian art that I had no interest in, but at least it was free. I think it's free cos they have so much of it. If there was just a few old pots

on show it would feel more special, but they had rows and rows of old pots, plates and jugs. They must have discovered an old Chinese version of Ikea buried somewhere.

We saw the Statue of Liberty from a distance, which I convinced myself was the best way to see it. We walked round Central Park and saw a bit of the zoo that you can see without paying. I do that at London Zoo. I think it annoys the zoo keepers, but they have a problem hiding the giraffes. We tried to get into the Empire State Building cos we thought that might have been free as well, but we couldn't find the entrance. No wonder King Kong climbed up the side of it. We spent the rest of the day looking for cheap delis that did "all you can eat" type offers.

It wasn't a great way to end a holiday. We were hungry and tired, and I didn't sleep well cos of all the noise. "New York, New York – so good they named it twice" … or was it because you didn't hear it the first time.

Malaga

The following are extracts from my diary.

February 9th

Got up at 5 a.m. to get to Heathrow as I'm going to see me mam and dad in Malaga. They've started going abroad in winter to get away from the miserable weather. They normally only pay around £400 for a month. The place they got last year wasn't that good – the power kept going off and the apartment faced a swamp.

Got on the Heathrow Express. I tried to sleep but couldn't cos they were showing a video about places to visit around the world. The presenter was somewhere where they have an annual event which involves having oranges chucked at your head. If that's the main attraction, it ain't worth going. I don't like having sticky orange juice all over me. I only eat oranges when I'm in the bath so I can dunk me hands after I've eaten them.

Met me mam and dad at airport. The apartment was alright. We went for a walk down the beach and saw a blind man. We talked about how much enjoyment he'd get out of being on the beach. I didn't think he'd like it that much cos the sand is all uneven. He was wearing dark glasses. I said it was odd that he was wearing shades as the only perk of being blind is that you don't have to wear glasses to keep the sun out of your eyes. I said they could move all blind people to really grim-looking places and bring in a load of birds that will tweet a lot and make it sound like they're in a really nice country area. Suzanne said this wouldn't be right.

We got back and put the telly on. It only picked up Spanish programmes, so we just played cards.

February 10th
Got up and had breakfast. We had Spanish sausages and egg. The sausages were nice. Me dad said they were only 60p for a pick of 15.

The news was on the telly but it was in Spanish. There was something about how the Chinese won't be eating whale anymore. Cos it was in Spanish, I don't know if it's cos they're not allowed or cos they are sick of it.

The Chinese eat some weird stuff. I used to cut through China Town in London quite a lot and I'd see odd things hanging up in the window. Duck's tongue was proudly on display. I can safely say that I've never had an urge to eat tongue, and if I did I don't think I'd pick a duck's. I didn't even know they had a tongue. The Chinese waste nothing. They are so different to us, even down to the way they print their books, which they do back to front. If I moved over there, I'd keep forgetting that and would read the end of every story by mistake. I once read that when someone dies in China, they sometimes don't get buried until a person they know also dies, so they can be buried together and won't be lonely in the afterlife. Like I say, they're odd the Chinese.

We went to a place me dad found that does coffee for 70 cents. None of us had coffee though.

Went to a supermarket to get some more cheap sausages. Me mam saw a birdcage in a pet shop that she wanted. Me dad said she couldn't have it cos it would be a pain to get on the plane with it.

We went back home and had a brew and played scrabble. The biggest word I got was equips. Suzanne put the word equip down but I put the S on the end.

Went for a drink in an English pub. We met up with a cousin that I hadn't seen for 27 years.

We got back home and me mam annoyed me dad cos she was still going on about the cage she wanted to buy for her parrot. Me dad said the parrot could be dead by the time they get home. Me mam didn't laugh cos she still hasn't got over the budgie dying at Christmas.

February 11th

Went for a walk round a harbour. There were some massive fish in big groups. Me mam fed them some bread. Me dad went mad when he realised it was from the sandwiches that she'd made us. He found out because she started chucking them a bit of one of the chocolate biscuits that were also for us. They ate the chocolate biscuit, which was weird. I think this is more proof that animals are changing their eating habits. When I was at work last year, having a roast dinner on the roof, a wasp came and nicked a bit of chicken off me plate and flew off with it. Wasps should not be eating roast chicken.

February 12th

Going home today. Me mam showed me something in one

of her ghost magazines that she brought with her. It was a yellow star that you had to rub and make a wish. Me mam said she rubbed it before we arrived and wished for good weather for us and it had worked. There was also a column about a woman who speaks to the dead. The woman said she'd been speaking to someone called Val, who died 4 years ago. Val had dark curly hair and a nice smile. It's odd how these people who talk to the dead never say anything horrible about them. You never get one saying "I'm getting an ugly cross-eyed woman with a fat arse."

It said if you knew Val you could get more information by calling the number. Me mam said it might have been Val who used to live on our estate. Me dad read it and told her not to be calling cos it cost £1.20 a minute.

Me dad took us to the airport. It started to rain.

They are staying for one more week. Me mam said she wishes she was going home cos she's had enough now and she misses the parrot.

Got on the plane and was sat next to a pilot who lived in Malaga and was heading to London to fly a plane to Boston. I used this opportunity to ask him if there are any pilots with rough accents as I've never heard one. He said no and then said he was going to the toilet. I never saw him again.

RELAXIN WITH ME DAD.

SOMEWHERE GRIM.

Sorrento

IF I WASN'T ENGLISH I'd probably like to be Italian. They seem to do the best food. I didn't have pasta until I was about 22 years old cos in our house we used to just have pie and chips, sausage egg and chips, chips beans and potato cakes, steak and chips, tomatoes and bacon, or mash and beans. I was quite happy with that choice but it just meant there was never any pasta. Suzanne's mam and dad still have the same food every week:

Monday	bacon and egg
Tuesday	sausage and chips
Wednesday	meat & potato pie and veg
Thursday	chops and veg

Friday	chippy
Saturday	ham sandwiches with sausage rolls
Sunday	Sunday roast (chicken or lamb)

So whatever day you're reading this, you'll know what they are cooking in their house.

Me Auntie Nora is the same. She'll prepare a week's worth of meals on a Sunday and then label 'em up with the days of the week. The daft thing is, I'll speak to her on say a Monday and ask what she's having for tea, and she'll say, "Oh I've prepared chilli for tonight but I don't fancy it." And I'll say, "Well eat what you've sorted out for Tuesday instead then", but she won't. She says it would mess up her schedule.

There's still loads of food I've not eaten. I don't see the point in rushing – I'll wait for a day when I'm bored of everything I've eaten and then try summat new. I still ain't had lobster. It looks like too much messing about. I was out once and saw someone order one and it came with a special tool to get into it. As far as I'm concerned, if you can't eat it with a knife and fork, that's a sign we shouldn't be eating it.

We went to a hotel in Sorrento and it was nice enough. The food was nice, but it does annoy me how there are so many different types of pasta. Just cos it's a different shape it's got a different name, but at the end of the day it still tastes the same. You shouldn't pick food based on its shape. I heard a while back that they were making square melons cos people got sick of the round ones rolling about the fridge. If I was a chicken, I'd be worried.

The hotel was in good condition and was clean enough. The only problem was that the place was full of old people. It was like I'd walked onto the set of *Cocoon*. At first I didn't think it would bother me cos I thought at least they'll be quiet and won't be coming in at all hours. But it was the other way round – they were getting up at all hours. I swear that one morning the people in the next room got up for breakfast when it was still dark.

This meant the other guests were out early and we could never get a chair by the pool, so we always ended up having to sit in the garden bit where all the wasps knocked about. I'd get my own back around 2 p.m. though, cos they'd all go in-doors and sit in the lounge and nod off in the big high-backed chairs, and we'd have a game of pool. You should have seen them jump in their chairs as the balls cracked as I broke.

Seeing as we didn't fancy getting up at 4 a.m. to get chairs round the pool, we spent a lot of time out of the hotel. We went to Pompeii on a coach trip. It was amazing. There was old stuff lying about everywhere (a bit like round the pool back at the hotel). A volcano went off about one thousand nine hundred years ago and wrecked the place, and it still ain't been cleaned up. There's still dust on top of stuff, old broken vases all over the place, and tracks in the road left from the chariots. There were even little rooms where prostitutes used to have it away with the fellas on these concrete beds, and the walls had all rude drawings on them which were quite well done. Normally old drawings only ever feature a yak being chased by a fella with a spear, so it was good to see an old doodle of a pair of tits and bloke with his nob out for a change.

The tour guide told us about the volcano. It's called Mount Vesuvius and is due to go off again soon. Our hotel was across the way from it, so for the rest of the week I kept a close eye on it. It reminded me of when I was younger and used to live across from a chemical plant. There was a flame that was always burning, 24 hours a day. Me brother told me that if the flame ever went out, the world would end. I used to sit at me window on windy nights being worried. I still don't know why the flame is always burning.

The old people in the hotel tanned really easily. I don't know why that happens. I think it's cos they hardly put any protection on. I saw some old fella rubbing a factor 3 on his wife's back, which is hardly worth the bother. The woman had loads of big brown moles on her back, which must have been caused by not putting on enough lotion. The fella was rubbing his hand in them all – it looked like he was swimming in Coco Pops. We decided to have another day out.

We booked a trip to Rome which included a night's accommodation. The coach was meant to pick us up at 8 a.m., so we were up early. Saying that, we were still the last ones up in the hotel. The coach was late. We always have this. The tour guide was being picked up at our hotel as well, and while we waited she talked to us about the volcano. They talk about that volcano in Sorrento like we talk about the weather in this country. "Yeah it's going to go off again soon", she said. It's funny how she knew that, yet she was clueless when it came to knowing when the coach would come. It turned up 45 minutes late.

It took ages to get to Rome but it was worth it. It's pretty amazing the amount of old stuff there is in Rome. Every corner you turn, there's another really old building. It ain't the place to live if you're a builder though, cos you'd never have any work. The more cracks in a building, the more the tourists love it. Some of 'em are in a right state. If the buildings were in Britain, they'd class them as dangerous structures and knock 'em down.

The only annoying thing about Rome was the amount of people hanging about dressed up as Romans and emperors. I saw a couple of them poking passers-by with their spears. Some of them were doing that thing where they stand really still and pretend to be a statue. I don't know why people take pictures of these as everyone looks really still in a photograph.

Even though I enjoyed Rome, I don't know if I'd go again as nothing changes there. They don't do anything up, they just leave it all to get older and older. It was really busy when we were there cos the Pope was out on his balcony. I suppose if I grew up in Rome I would be more into religion, cos having the Pope living down the road would make me more keen to know what he's going on about. If it's on your doorstep, you show more interest don't you? But because of where I grew up, I like *Coronation Street* instead.

We watched the Pope for a bit but not much was happening. It wasn't the current pope, it was the old one. I say the old one but the new one is also old. I don't know why they keep taking on really old people for the job. Me dad tried to get some part-time work at B&Q and was turned away for being too old, and yet the new Pope got the gig when he was 78, and me dad was only 63. It seems like it's one rule for one and one rule for another.

If you're still alive you can start Monday.

When we got to the hotel in Rome I thought it was some sort of special hotel for fitness freaks cos the bathroom was full of bars hanging from the ceiling and walls. Turns out it was a room for the elderly or disabled. That's the weird thing with Italy, There's more old stuff than new stuff, even with the people. I think the people live longer there. It might be because they are surrounded by really old stuff that never changes, so they are not reminded that they are getting old. Whereas in Britain old people are forever seeing big changes to places and saying "in my day it was all fields 'ere", which makes them feel old in the head and so they die. Just a theory.

ROME

Rome was not built in a day,
It just looks that way.

Cotswolds

The following are extracts from my diary.

March 12th

Got up early to take Suzanne to the Cotswolds for her birthday. It was freezing. The weather said there was a chance of snow. We picked up the car from the hire place and set off.

We found the B&B really easily. Problem was we were early and our room wasn't ready, so we had to go for a walk. There wasn't much around the B&B so we ended up just having a walk around the car park.

When we went back in, the room was ready. It was nice but quite old looking. It had flower patterns everywhere.

We had a view of the car park we'd just walked around. There were coat hangers in the wardrobe with sponge on them to protect your clothes. I think this is an unnecessary invention. I saw a good invention that I thought I'd buy me mam the other day. It was a pair of slippers with lights on the front. She'd like them cos she always stays up really late playing the games on the Sky box. She always goes upstairs when she's finished without putting the light on cos she doesn't want to wake me dad up. I think they were £29, batteries included.

We booked a table for a Sunday roast and went to see if there was anything other than the car park to walk round. We found a field that was a bird sanctuary but we couldn't see any birds on it, so we went to the pub.

We had our dinner in the B&B. It was nice but there was a loud family of about 13 people sat behind us. I've never seen the point in going out in large numbers. One of the family asked for sorbet for a starter. He was only about 11. He thought he was it. Kids know too much these days, they've got nothing to live for. Sorbet is another food that I didn't have until I was in me twenties. I said I'd had enough and needed a kip, so we went back to the room. I ate the free biscuits and slept for two hours.

We went down to the bar around 7:30. Luckily the big

family weren't there but we managed to sit down near an old couple. One of 'em was a bit deaf. She was shouting to her husband saying how her strawberries were awful. Her husband agreed. Weird though, cos when I went to the bar I noticed they'd managed to eat them all.

We looked at the events board on the way to our room to see if there was anything worth doing before we leave tomorrow. There was just one leaflet about the bird sanctuary but we'd already seen that. Went back to the room and watched *Planet Earth*. They filmed a panda for four weeks and all it did was sit in its hole. It did nowt. If I was Fiat I'd stop naming one of my cars a Fiat Panda. It suggests it won't move much. It would be like having a Ford Sloth. No one would buy it.

March 13th

Didn't sleep that well cos the bed had sheets instead of a quilt. We got up and rushed down for breakfast cos they stopped serving it at 8:30. I had poached egg and toast.

It was a bit warmer today so we drove into the next village and had a walk round. We did the usual sort of thing. We looked in estate agents' windows to see how much the houses were round there and then walked round the graveyard to see who could find the oldest dead person. There was one there from 1894.

We drove to the next village. It only had a post office. It was shut. It also had 3 ducks. We found a pub that was open so we went in there and had some dinner. It was a really old pub that had the original floor in it. Some tourists were taking a picture of it.

It took three hours to drive back to London. People say they go to the country to see the wildlife. On the way back I saw three hedgehogs, a fox and a rabbit. All dead on the road. I also saw a dead badger. I've never seen a living badger. Always dead.

Suzanne never said but I think she enjoyed her birthday night away.

Weymouth

The following are extracts from my diary.

July 11th

Suzanne has been working away for a few weeks, so she booked us a week in Weymouth. We got up early and had an argument. I caused it. I hadn't cleaned any underpants while she was away, so I didn't have any to take with me. I said I'd buy some on the way.

We left early cos there is a gay parade on in London today. Last time they had one of these it caused problems on the tube cos there were loads of drag queens who couldn't walk up the stairs in their high heels. I remember seeing a fella last year who was rushing to be at the start of the parade. He was rushing down Wardour Street on a bike whilst wearing high heels and a miniskirt. He looked gormless all glammed up while wearing a cycling helmet.

I bought some underpants in Richmond. I think it's the first time I've ever bought underpants. I normally wait till someone buys me some for a present for Christmas or my birthday. It's the same with tea towels. I bought a pack of four for £5.99. I don't think you can buy one underpant.

We got to the place we were staying at by 4 p.m. The room was basic but OK. I ate the free biscuits and then we had a quick walk down the beach. There were loads of kids on it looking for fossils. Apparently a lot of dinosaurs died round here. There were signs on the beach asking people not to take the pebbles as some of them are between 60 and 150 million years old. Pebbles all look the same age to me. They're like pigeons.

We had our tea in the restaurant downstairs. We thought the food and service were gonna be bad cos the fella on the next table seemed to be sighing all the time. Turned out he had a breathing problem. The food was good.

July 12th

Slept well but was woken by people upstairs cos the floor was squeaky. When we went downstairs to get breakfast the people from upstairs were on their way out. They were proper walkers. They had maps round their necks on string and had waterproof clothes on. It was a really sunny day, so I don't know how far they were planning on walking.

We had breakfast and then drove to another beach. We paddled in the sea. There was a big fish that had been washed up. It was dead. It's eyes were missing. I asked Suzanne if any fish just die of old age or are they all just eaten by other fish and caught by fisherman. She said she didn't know in that "I'm not listening" sort of way.

We went to another beach where there was a big rock with a hole in it. Loads of people were standing in the hole having their picture taken. There were signs on the rock asking people not to climb on it as it could cave in. This annoys me as they've had ages to fix it cos it says it's been here for 160 million years.

There was a gift shop selling postcards and little orna-ments of the rock with a hole in. Loads of people were buying them. It's the sort of the thing that me Auntie Nora would buy. She's got loads of ornaments. Me mam told me that the last time she stayed over at Nora's she couldn't sleep so she got up. She ended up counting all of her ornaments in the lounge and morning room. She said there was 327.

We went from there to a lighthouse that the kids cartoon *Portland Bill* is supposed to be based on. We didn't hang around there for long though as we hadn't eaten all day and I was starting to feel weak. I think I've got a touch of diabetes. I bought a chunky KitKat and headed back.

We spent £14 on parking today. No wonder the tourist industry in this country is on its arse.

July 13th

Was woken by the radio alarm clock at 7:30. It shocked me. It was the buzzer on it that went off. I don't know why anyone would choose to be woken up by that buzzer. I had palpitations for about 20 minutes. I reckon it's taken some time off me life.

We went down for breakfast. There were people down there we hadn't seen before cos we weren't up as early yesterday. There was an old couple who were sat at a table with what looked like four of their grand kids. The gran was doing all the organising and ordering of the food, but the grandad just sat there looking fed up. I think he was deaf. He just sat there looking at the brown sauce bottle. None of them were involving him.

It was a cloudy day so I said we should go to Monkey World. They've got every sort of monkey going in there. I never thought I'd say this, but I was sick of the sight of them.

Sometimes you can have too much of a good thing. There was also too many old people in mobility vehicles. You couldn't get close to the fences to look at the chimps cos the old people had created a sort of convoy. There was one woman who must have been about 110 who was being pushed around by her daughter, who looked about 80. She didn't have a clue where she was. I don't know why the daughter had wasted £9 of her pension getting her mam in there. She would have been just as happy left in the car park.

We went and sat by the sea and ate some chips. There was a tarot card reader in a tent on the beach. There were loads of good write-ups stuck on a board outside the tent, with stories about lottery winners who got their numbers from the woman in the tent and people with illnesses that she cured. It said if you could prove she was a fake she'd give you £1000. I was close to giving it ago when I noticed she was sat outside having her lunch. She was eating a hot dog. It ruined the whole mysticalness.

In a way I was glad I didn't have it done. I don't want to know my future. There's hardly any surprises these days – we're told everything. I try and avoid it all. I even turn the weather forecast off cos it's nice to wake up in the morning and see what the weather's like as you open the curtains.

I liked our break in Weymouth.

ONE OF MANY WALKS AROUND GRAVEYARDS. I THINK I CAUGHT AN ORB ON THIS ONE.

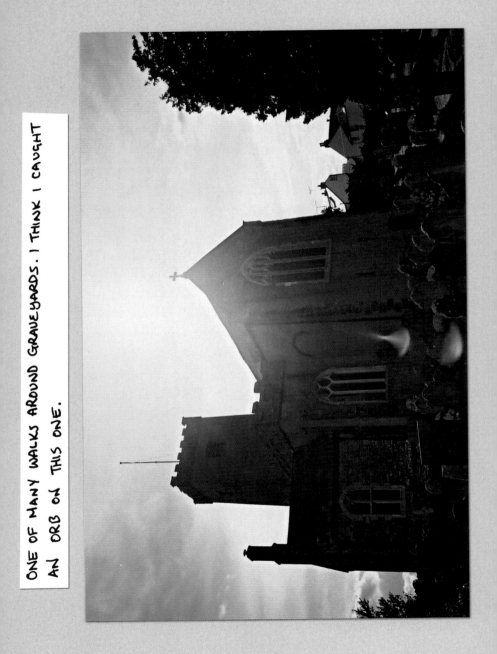

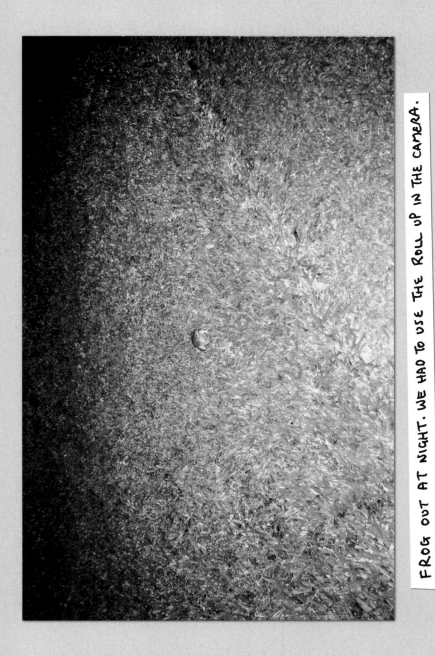

FROG OUT AT NIGHT. WE HAD TO USE THE ROLL UP IN THE CAMERA.

BANK HOLIDAY MONDAY

Bank holiday Monday
Bank holiday mundane
No shops open
Plenty of rain

Caribbean

PROBLEM WITH THE CARIBBEAN IS, the rooms are always too close to the sea for my liking. All it takes is for a ship to go past and cause a wave and it would have wiped out our room. It's the only place I've been where I've thought about going to bed wearing armbands.

It's mad how clean the sea is in the Caribbean. It's as if the sea in the rest of the world is a big council estate for poor fish, while the Caribbean is for the rich fish. Even though I don't really like the sea, it's hard to resist going in it in the Caribbean. I hadn't been in for years, but when I went to St Lucia I took the gamble.

First of all I just went in up to me knees and got out, then I went in up to me waist and got out, and then I finally went in and had a swim. I got out after 20 minutes feeling refreshed and sat in the sun. Ten minutes later I was hot again and said to Suzanne that I was gonna go back in. She stayed on her lounger. Here I was going back in the sea for the second time in an hour, after about 20 years of not going in it at all. I was thinking what an idiot I'd been when I got a really really really really sharp pain on me foot.

It was like the top of me foot had been slashed by broken glass. I turned round and ran out of the sea and went back to Suzanne. My feet are normally a size 10. My left foot still was, but my right foot was now a size 12. It had ballooned and had red streaks all over the top of it. Suzanne asked if I'd seen what did it. I hadn't. It came from nowhere. It was like I'd been happyslapped from some yob fish that had come from the rough part of the sea I mentioned earlier.

I should never have gone in. There's way too much weird stuff floating about in the sea. There's some octopus that's the size of a ten pence piece and can kill you if it touches you. It's got eight arms, so the chance of it touching you is pretty high. Like I said, too much weird dangerous stuff.

Suzanne said it might have been a jellyfish and told me I should get some ice. I had to queue at the bar for five minutes before being told I couldn't have any ice as there was a wedding on and they needed it all for the fruit punch.

There was a wedding every day in our hotel. I think people have this idea that it will be really romantic to get married there, but it isn't cos everyone stands around watching. We watched a couple tie the knot around the pool area. There they were getting to the serious "I do" bit when a fella from

Scotland who was in the pool did a huge burp while his brother stood watching with his hands down his trunks. Hardly the stuff you read in Mills & Boon, is it?

There was supposed to be a gay wedding on the day we were going home. A fella I was sat next to on the beach – a printer from Milton Keynes – thought this was outrageous. He asked me what I thought and I said whose surname do they keep? He didn't discuss it with me any more after that.

Anyway, the fella behind the bar said I'd be okay but should see the hotel doctor, who was at lunch but would be back at some point. That's the problem with the Caribbean – everyone is too chilled. The jellyfish that stung me was probably just trying to give me a high five. I ended up getting two fruit punches and taking the ice out of them. I wrapped it in a towel and held it on me foot. I saw the doctor two hours later. He used a cotton wool ball to wipe me foot with alcohol and told me not to wear socks for 24 hours. You don't hear that sort of advice on *Casualty* do you?

We did a couple of trips while we were there. It was a bit sad cos an old woman died in apartment 20, but her husband still went on the trip they'd booked. We did a tour of the island by car. In one of the places we stopped at, the guide pointed out a cashew tree and told us not to eat the nuts hanging from it as they are poisonous when untreated. I couldn't see what he was pointing out as there was a massive German woman on our tour who was blocking my view. I asked Suzanne what it looked like so I don't go eating it. She just told me not to eat anything off a tree.

The tour included a BBQ on a small private beach that we could only get to by kayak. The kayaks had two seats on them. The guide suggested that the women should sit at the back and do the steering while the blokes sat in the middle and did the rowing. The only people who didn't do it this way round were the big German woman, whose husband was smaller than her so they swapped places, and the old fella whose wife had died – he shared a kayak with the tour guide.

The place we had to kayak from was pretty rank and we had to go through a type of Amazon jungle. The guide said there was nothing dangerous in the water but someone noticed hundreds of jellyfish. The guide said something about how they don't sting as they don't realise they can. I was a bit worried cos there must be one clever one among them who knows they can sting. They can't all be daft. I picked one up with my oar. It looked really odd and ill cos of the muddy waters they live in. Their morale must be pretty low, looking the way they do. That's probably why they don't sting. They probably think they are good for nothing.

Me and Suzanne were no good at kayaking and ended up having an argument cos I couldn't row properly. The only people behind us were the big German woman and her husband. She weighed her kayak down at the back, which meant her fella was struggling to row. They lost balance and tipped over into the muddy waters. She really struggled to get back on. Her face went red and she was having problems breathing as she cocked her leg up, giving us a view of thick mud spilling from her bikini round her arse.

Twenty minutes later we were there. We were all knackered. Instead of talking about the lovely beach and views, everyone was talking tactics on how to kayak back. I say everyone, but the German woman was out in the sea scooping mud out of her arse with one hand while eating a chicken leg with the other.

It's weird how holidays are meant to be relaxing and yet people always do more active stuff when they're away. When I was in Tunisia I'd have a kip around 3 p.m. cos the heat made me tired, and every day I'd be woken by some holiday rep shouting at a row of 80-year-olds, who he had doing star-jumps to the music of Chaka Demus & Pliers. How none of them died I do not know. Normally at this time of day they'd be relaxed in front of the telly, eating a tea cake while waiting for *Countdown* to come on.

I've never been into exercise. I don't think the body is supposed to be pushed to the max – I think people just do it for the recognition. When I used to live in Docklands in London I once had to move from my flat to another one just down the road. I decided that I didn't need a removal van as I could carry the stuff on my own. The day I moved turned out to be the day of the London Marathon. There I was walking down Westferry Road with a lamp in one hand and a magazine rack in the other, and all the spectators thought I was doing some sort of novelty fun run and were clapping. It made me feel quite good, but not good enough to want to train 15 hours a day.

I watched some event on the telly where the people in-

volved had to run a couple of miles, jump into a river and swim for about 5 minutes, jump on a bike and pedal up a hill, and then run for another five minutes to the finish line. The winner got a gold medal – the same prize that the winner of the 100 metres got. So why not just do that?

We ate the chicken and then I sat on the beach while Suzanne did a bit of snorkelling. I didn't fancy it after the jellyfish incident. I sat and listened to an annoying loud woman who was telling another couple where they should visit and where they should eat on the island. She was saying how she'd been here for two weeks and had another week to go. She kept bossing her husband around – she had him up and down getting chicken for the couple she was talking to, then she had him rubbing suntan lotion on her back, and then he had to shift the plates of chicken bones cos they were attracting wasps. She was a right pain in the arse. Her husband didn't really chat. He just sat there with his shades on pretending to read, but I know he was eyeing up the younger women in their swimming gear cos I watched him for ten minutes and he didn't turn a page once.

We got back on the kayak. Me and Suzanne did OK going back. We came second to the tour guide and the fella whose wife had died the day before. I think we would have let him win anyway.

JELLYFISH

I don't like jellyfish, they're not a fish, they're just a blob.
They don't have eyes, fins or scales like a cod.
They float about blind, stinging people in the seas,
And no one eats jellyfish with chips and mushy peas.
Get rid of 'em.

Lanzarote

PEOPLE SAY that when you buy someone a present, you should buy them something they wouldn't buy for themselves. The first time I experienced this was when my Auntie Nora gave me a T-shirt for my eighth birthday with a black-and-white image of her face on the front of it. The second time was when Suzanne booked us a week in Lanzarote for my Christmas present. I definitely wouldn't have paid to go there myself.

The holiday didn't start well. Twenty minutes into the flight there was a call asking if there was a doctor on board. As always, there was. I don't know why doctors and nurses are always going on strike for being overworked and not having enough days off, as they always seem to be going on holiday. Saying that, if I was a doctor and the captain asked if there was a doctor on board, I think I'd keep my mouth shut. It doesn't seem fair that you get hassled when you're supposed to be off. I was once on a flight to Copenhagen and one of the toilets was out of order, but they didn't go hassling any plumbers on board.

The flight went back to Stansted and the ill passenger got off. She was an old woman who was having dizzy spells.

Four hours later we were on a coach on the way to our hotel in the pouring rain. The rep, a chubby girl with curly hair from Yorkshire, was stood at the front with a microphone giving us a load of information. All I remember her saying was that it had been the wettest December in years and that the movie *Planet of the Apes* was filmed on the island. I wasn't really listening to her, I was more interested in listening to the Scottish couple sat behind us. They were telling the people next to them how they'd been up since 2:30 this morning getting from Glasgow to Stansted and how they only booked the holiday two days ago and are being allocated a hotel on arrival. The woman was saying how it's the best way of doing it cos you get the best deals that way. She went on to say how she needs to have cheap holidays as she's saving to have some work done on her face.

They were dropped off first. The place looked pretty

grim. I think they were dropped off first so they didn't get to see how nice the other places that people would be staying at were. As they got off I had a look of them. The woman looked like Gordon Ramsay with tattoos. She has a lot saving to do.

We were at our hotel 30 minutes later. It was massive. It looked clean enough though, mainly due to the rain that was seeping down the walls and under the doors. As Suzanne signed us in I watched the hotel staff stuffing beach towels under the doors to stop the rain coming in. There were families sat around the reception area with their cases, smoking as many fags as they could before their flight home. They didn't look very tanned, but looked quite happy to be leaving.

I could hear some tribute act singing songs by The Supremes in the family room. One of the staff was called away from making a dam with towels to carry our cases to our room. I said I could manage, but the reception staff said we'd have a problem finding it on our own, even though she'd given us a map of the hotel grounds and marked where the room was. They were right, we would never have found it. We had to go through six doors, up four floors in a lift, past two pools, and then up a few more stairs to our room. Room number 355. There were crowbar marks around the door lock, which I thought would be a nice reminder if we forgot the room number.

We sat on the bed and looked at the map of the hotel. It was huge. They should have given us a compass when we signed in. We thought we'd have an early night, so we'd have the energy to walk to the canteen area in the morning.

The eating area was down in the basement. It was a big L-shaped room with lime-green walls lit by about 30 fluorescent tube lights that flickered. Probably due to the rain that had seeped through onto the electrics. It was self-service and seated about 200 people. There was only one toaster. People were having their picture taken next to a big mound of something that we thought was butter that had been made to look like a volcano.

Lanzarote is a volcanic island, so everywhere is pretty grey and dusty. It's like one big ashtray. We tried to go on as many trips as we could just to get us out of the hotel, and all of them involved something to do with volcanoes. Now, I do find them amazing, but after seeing about eight I'd had enough. At the end of the day they're just holes.

After seeing about another 20 holes we were taken to a house that once belonged to a local artist, César Manrique. He built his house under the hardened lava from the volcanoes. Saying that, it still had more natural light than the canteen back at the hotel. The tour guide said she would allow us an hour to have a walk round the house. We were done after about 25 minutes. It wasn't a big place. Here we were in the middle of nowhere, surrounded by old lava and with another 40 minutes to kill. They said the house was preserved as it was when César lived there. There was just one change – a tuck shop that sold overpriced food and drink and bits of lava. So this is why we were given an hour, the tour guide must have been getting a backhander from the person who ran the place. Captive audience. Suzanne said she wanted a drink but I said no cos it's a con.

Five minutes after leaving Mr Manrique's house, the coach pulled up at a roundabout. The guide told everyone that this is where César was knocked down and killed. She then gave us a few minutes to get off and take photos of where he was hit. We didn't get off the coach as it was obviously a dangerous road.

The guide said she'd saved the best part till last. The coach started to make it's way up a big hill. She turned off her mic and the driver turned on the tape deck – it was the theme from *2001: A Space Odyssey*. I think the idea was that as the music built to the big finale, we'd turn a corner at the top of the hill and see something amazing. But due to the amount of other coaches going up the hill, plus the tight corners, he had to pause the theme tune. It was replaced with the "vehicle reversing horn". He then pressed play again but he'd mistimed it and had to put his foot down to catch up. The coach was screeching round the edge of the cliff and everyone was looking a bit worried. We got to the top but the music finished about 3 seconds too soon, and the amazing bit was revealed with a backing track of hiss from the worn-out old tape. The driver looked well fed up. Anyway, the "amazing" thing was another bloody volcano. The difference with this one was that there was an expert chucking water down it. Four seconds later a jet of steam would come shooting out. We were given 45 minutes to take photos.

Christmas Day was a bit depressing. Most people had gone back home on Christmas Eve. We started the day by going for breakfast, avoiding big piles of shit on the way. It turned out

to be camel shit. There were five of them in the hotel grounds with fellas dressed as Father Christmas on the back of them.

There wasn't much going on in the hotel, apart from a free back wax for all guests. A lot of people had it done just cos it was free. For

£10 you could have back, sack and crack done. I've never understood why they sell it in that order. If I had it done I'd change the order to sack, crack and back. I'm guessing it hurts most on the sack, so get that out the way first, then move on to the crack or even just do one long wax strip from crack to back. Anyway, we didn't take advantage of the free offer and went for breakfast.

I had some toast for the first time since arriving, as the queue for the toaster wasn't too bad, and then we had a wander down the beach. Everything was going well until we stopped looking out to the sea and started to look at the people around us. They were all stark bollock naked. It was a nudist beach. An old fella who looked about 79 walked past us. He wasn't totally naked. He wore a hat and glasses and flip-flops, he had a big rucksack on his back, and he was smoking a pipe. He gave me a nod as he passed. I don't know if it was his flip-flops that were making the slapping sound or his balls slapping on his legs.

I told Suzanne we're not going any further and turned round and headed back. We passed more nude people. There was a woman who came walking out of the sea with a mental amount of pubic hair. It looked like she was smuggling seaweed out of the sea. Her husband sat on the beach looking embarrassed. He wasn't naked. I wondered if he knew she was into getting naked before they went on holiday cos he didn't look happy. We had to walk back at a slower pace than normal cos we kept getting too close to the old naked man who wore flip-flops and had a dimpled arse. I really don't understand what it's all about.

That evening we saw the old fella in the canteen. This time he was overdressed. He had a shirt and tie with blazer, long trousers and sandals with socks. He looked younger with clothes on.

On the plane home I saw the woman who looked like Gordon Ramsay. She was really tanned. People who aren't that good looking always tend to tan well.

LANZAROTE. I PAID MONEY TO SEE THIS

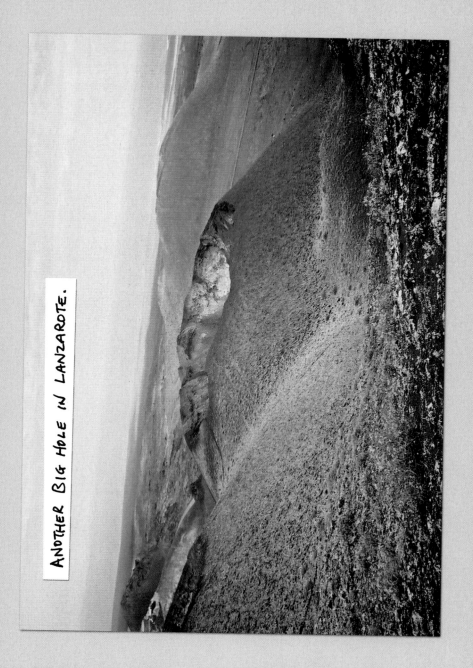

ANOTHER BIG HOLE IN LANZAROTE.

SCIENTIFIC EXPERIMENT IN LANZAROTE

DON'T KNOW WHERE I AM OR WHY WE TOOK THIS PICTURE.

Madeira

The following are extracts from my diary.

September 30th

Going away with Suzanne's mam and dad. We are meeting them at Madeira airport as they are flying in from Manchester.

It's meant to be relaxing going on holiday, so why do the flights start so early. We had to get up at 3:45 a.m. to get to the airport. I felt sick on the train on the way.

The flight was delayed due to some drunk fella who had pushed his girlfriend over. She was crying and his mam was shouting at him saying, "She's sick of you ruining holidays!" He was told to get off the plane and his mam and girlfriend went on their own.

The plane was full and I had a headache. There was a baby sat behind us that was crying its eyes out for the whole flight. The mother said it was upset cos its ears were hurting. So were mine.

We hung about for 20 minutes near the baggage carousel waiting to meet Suzanne's mam and dad, cos that's what we'd arranged to do. Turned out they had already arrived but decided to wait outside cos they wanted a fag.

We had to get two cabs to the villa cos they couldn't fit five of us into one. They cost 85 euros each.

The villa is okay. It has a small pool that is about 15 ft x 5 ft. It has a portable telly and a rocking chair. We had a cup of tea. Suzanne's dad brought his own teabags. It took ages to make as the kettle isn't electric.

October 1st

Got woken up at 7 a.m. by the church that faces our room. I still have a headache.

Suzanne's mam had her own bedroom cos Suzanne's dad snores too loudly. She wasn't happy with her bedroom as the traffic was keeping her awake. Suzanne said she can swap with us. I didn't tell her about the church bells.

Suzanne's dad said he liked the free biscuits that were

in the cupboard. They were a Portuguese version of Rich Tea.

We went to try and find a supermarket. Suzanne's mam was having a go at her dad cos he didn't have a shirt on. She said he looks a mess and is embarrassed to be seen with him. It's their ruby anniversary tomorrow.

Me and Suzanne stayed in tonight cos I had heatstroke. We watched a foreign version of *Deal Or No Deal* on the portable. You don't need to hear what's being said on that programme to understand it.

October 2nd

Didn't sleep well due to mopeds on the main road. If it wasn't the mopeds it was the springs in the bed. Suzanne's mam said she didn't sleep well again cos of the church bells. She wants to swap rooms with Suzanne's dad tonight. She thinks she's bleedin' Goldilocks.

We had to go and buy some toilet rolls and water. I got Suzanne to buy some soap for her mam cos she kept using ours. She kept nicking Suzanne's suntan lotion as well. I don't know what she brought in that big bloody case of hers.

I bought a fan to put in our room to drown out the sound of the mopeds. I've heard Wayne Rooney does the same thing with a vacuum cleaner.

We went out for tea. We let Suzanne's mam and dad pick cos it was their anniversary. They picked an Irish pub that sold sausage and chips (cos it was a Tuesday).

We went back and watched *Jerry Maguire* in Spanish. Suzanne wanted to go to bed but I said I just wanted to hear the "Show me the money" line in Spanish to see if it's as catchy. It wasn't.

October 3rd

Didn't do much this morning. Just sat by the pool saving insects that flew into it. It was full of death. There were three wasps drowned on the bottom.

Went and watched people being dragged down a hill in some sort of bread basket. It's something they do here for the tourists. We didn't bother having a go.

We walked round the shops. Suzanne's dad bought two packets of the biscuits he liked to take back home with him. Suzanne's mam bought a tin of corned beef.

It was a bit of a boring day today.

October 4th

A bloke turned up today to check if everything had been okay for us. Suzanne's dad said it would have been handy if there had been a plastic draining board. The fella was Portuguese and didn't understand. I think an electric kettle was more of a priority. I couldn't be bothered mentioning it though as we are off home tomorrow.

There was a dead bird out the back. Suzanne's dad said it looks like it flew into the wall and killed itself. Loads of ants were eating it. I dug a hole under a tree and buried it. The ants were still all hanging around the scene of death ages after the burial. Suzanne's dad said I should have left the bird for the ants to eat cos I was messing up the food chain. I felt bad so I gave the ants some breadcrumbs.

We have to eat all the food we've got cos we're going home tomorrow.

Suzanne's mam cut her finger opening the corned beef tin and fainted. We think it's cos she went and drank the free bottle of local port that was in the welcome pack.

Tunisia

WE WERE GREETED by a midget. This word isn't used as much these days as it's classed as being a bit nasty and you're meant to say "little person", but I want you to know that when I say "little person" I mean a really little person and not just someone who is small.

He offered to carry our cases. I wanted to say, "no it's okay, I'll carry them", but then I thought that would be like saying he's not capable. So I let him do it. It took him eight minutes to get the cases to our room.

He did the quick tour of the room. He described everything as big. "You have a big bed", "big bathroom to your right", "big balcony through here". I don't know if that was the way they were told to sell the rooms to guests, or if he was just saying that cos to him everything was BIG.

It was all a bit tatty. It wasn't long after he'd left that I was on the phone to reception asking for maintenance. There was a problem with the water – for some reason the shower would only run hot water if the lights in the bathroom were on. The main desk said they would send someone up.

Twenty minutes later there was a knock at the door. It was another little person. A different little person from the one that brought the cases. This one had overalls on and had a BIG spanner. I told him my problem. He said that this was one of the older, cheaper rooms. He said he knew this cos of the fact we didn't have a TV. I said I'm not that concerned about not having a TV, unless having one meant that turning it on would give us hot water. He ran the shower and then used the spanner to reach up and flick the light switch. The water went cold. He then jumped up and hit the switch again and it went warm. He said, "If the water doesn't go warm when the light is on, call reception" and off he went.

We went for tea down in the buffet area and were asked what we'd like to drink by ANOTHER little person. I wondered if it was some sort of theme or if they just took on all these small people so the hotel looked bigger in the brochure. This little fella annoyed me as he was trying it on with Suzanne. He kissed her hand and pinched her arse. I said, "Right, less of that." Everyone around the buffet area looked at me like I was evil. It's annoying how people look down their noses at you if you have an argument with someone who isn't as able-bodied as yourself. Disabled people don't mind, but able-bodied people say, "oh leave 'em alone", even when the disabled person is in the wrong.

I once got on a train from Manchester to London that was chock-a-block. People were standing in the aisles and sitting on the floor near the toilets. I looked down the carriage and noticed two empty seats at a table. I climbed over people and made my way to them. I sat down and a voice from across the table said hello.

I said hello back. It was a young lad with Down's syndrome. He was talking to people but they were all ignoring him, which I thought was a bit rude. He turned to me and said loudly, "You're muscly."

"Cheers", I said back.

"Why?"

"Why what?"

"Why are you muscly?"

I didn't know what to say to that. I didn't think I was muscly. I thought he was more muscly than me. I decided the easiest way to get through this was to lie.

"I go to the gym", I said. I thought it was a good answer. I thought he'd be happy with that, and that would be the end of it.

"Arm wrestle me", he said.

People who were ignoring him before were now looking up from behind their books and magazines.

"Me arms ache a bit from all the gym work I did last night", I said.

"Arm wrestle!" He said it louder this time.

This is the bit that proves my point. The people on the train were looking at me like I was being mean cos I wouldn't arm wrestle him.

"Arm wrestle! Arm wrestle!"

I arm wrestled him.

I won't bother going into who won the arm wrestle cos it's not important. What really annoyed me was the fact that the fella who was meant to be looking after him was sat in first class and only popped in now and again to make sure he wasn't hassling anyone. People smiled admiringly when the man came and yet it wasn't him that was sat there keeping the lad entertained.

"You behaving yourself, George? Here you go, here's a can of beer. See you in a bit." And off he went back to first class.

The beer seemed to calm him down and he ended up talking to me about how he liked to eat Chinese and sausages but couldn't have too many of them cos they weren't good for his heart.

Anyway, after I told the little fella in Tunisia to stop pinching Suzanne's arse he steered clear of us and went and harassed some other woman guest.

The next morning we had a greeting meeting in a discotheque that was joined to our hotel. It was a dark, dingy place with carpet on the walls. At the time that seemed quite odd, but it doesn't any more. I think that's due to the fact that I wallpapered over a big mirror in our flat. It's only a small flat and the fella who owned it before us thought that having a mirror on the wall would make it feel bigger. I didn't think it did. It just made it look more messy cos if the room was a mess, you could see the mess twice. I looked at taking it down but was told it might rip the plaster off the wall, so I left it up and wallpapered over it. When I tell people, they look at me like I'm daft, but I think it looks alright. I just have to remember not to nail any pictures up.

So, we had our greeting meeting and were told the usual stuff like "don't flush too much toilet paper down the toilet" and "make sure you drink lots of water", and then we were told a few facts about the place. The rep said a lot of films had been filmed in Tunisia. "Can you name any?" she said. One of the guests said *Life of Brian* and *Star Wars.* She said he was correct and that you could add *Raiders of the Lost Ark* to the list as well. I was gonna have a punt on *Charlie and the Chocolate Factory*, with all the little fellas knockin' about.

There were a couple of day trips to places used in the films, but we didn't bother going. I didn't see the point. Instead we went to Sousse, the nearby town. From the moment we got out the taxi we were hassled by the locals to buy their stuff. Leather jackets, wallets, bags and sandals made from lizard skin. I'd never want shoes made from lizard skin – I don't think they sound that comfy. I remember thinking the same thing when Jimmy Nail sang about crocodile shoes.

I read something once about how the lizards were sick of being captured by the locals and made into shoes, so they got matey with the local scorpions. The lizards live in holes in the sand and the local people used to just stick their hands down the holes and grab them, so the lizards did a deal with the scorpions. They allowed them to use their holes as a home, as long as they guard the lizards. Along comes a local man thinking about making some nice lizard flip-flops, finds a lizard hole, sticks his hand in, scorpion kills him. It amazes me how creatures sort stuff out. The locals have stopped doing it as much now, but this has put the price of the flip-flops up cos of the danger involved.

There was loads of odd creatures in Tunisia. I think it's cos of the heat. Me brother said he noticed the same thing in Cyprus – he said the flies there were that big, you couldn't fit them in a matchbox. I don't know why he was trying to. In Tunisia loads of weird flying cockroaches used to come out at night and fly into people. I don't think they should have had wings cos they didn't know how to use them. Moths are the same. I think it's mad how they don't have eyes and yet are given wings – it's an accident waiting to happen. The flying cockroaches were about the size of Murray Mints and would just fly into your clothes and then cling on. The first night I was there I thought all the women were wearing the same brooch, until I noticed they were moving. Every five minutes you'd hear a scream from some woman who had a cockroach on her jumper or in her hair.

I think cockroaches are the weirdest thing on the planet (next to jellyfish). They are the hardest of all creatures. I've read that they can hold their breath for 45 minutes and can live for a week without a head. Scientists say they would survive a nuclear attack as well. It's weird how insects are so different from each other and yet people are all the same. Cockroaches get all those super powers and then you get mayflies that only live one day. Seems a bit cruel to then go and name them after a month when they only live a day.

I don't see the point in some creatures either. I called an expert once and asked him if we really needed jellyfish. He didn't understand the question so I said, "If we got rid of all the jellyfish that are on the world, would it matter?" He said it would be very sad. I said, "Yeah but you're only saying that cos you work with 'em and you'd be jobless if they weren't about, but would it really matter if you got a call from someone who said that the last jellyfish on the world has just died?" After a long chat the only reason he came up with was that we need them cos turtles eat them. I said, "Yeah but turtles would find something else to eat in the same way that when I lived in Manchester I used to really like to eat some biscuits that were called Happy Faces but when I moved to London I couldn't find them anywhere so I found some new ones that I liked called Tunnock's Caramel Wafers." He said he had to go and hung up.

We didn't stay in Sousse for long and had two options for getting back to the hotel. There was the traditional taxi, which there didn't seem to be many of. Or a camel.

Suzanne didn't fancy the camel. I didn't either really, as I don't like to get on the back of animals that are bigger than me. I had a bad experience when I was about six. I had a go on a horse at a car-boot sale, and scruffy Sandra, a woman off the estate, accidentally burnt the horse's arse with her fag. It ran off at high speed with me on the back. The saddle slid round with me still in it, now getting kicked in the head by the horse. It eventually stopped and the woman offered me another free go. I didn't take her up on the offer.

We managed to get a taxi. It took a lot longer to get back to the hotel than it had taken to get to Sousse. Not because he took us a long way round, not because the traffic was bad, but because one of the taxi's wheels came off. It came undone and jammed under the wheel arch, putting the car into a skid. He didn't have a spare or any tools and told us we might be better off walking. We were in the middle of nowhere, about 90 degrees in the shade, with no water. Suzanne said we're not walking. We sat in the car and waited for another taxi to pass.

We ended up sharing one with a couple from Wiltshire. They were staying at the same hotel as us, which we thought was handy. Problem was, after sharing the taxi, whenever they saw us in the bar or round the pool they came and sat with us. All we'd done was share a cab but that was enough for them to think we were their holiday mates. I've always kept meself to meself on holidays cos as soon as you speak to someone, this is what happens. We'd pretend to be asleep on our deck chairs so they wouldn't stop to chat, but they'd just nudge us.

We didn't sit round the pool after that, we thought we'd go and hide on the beach. But we didn't get any peace there either. I'd thought the hard sell was bad in Sousse, but that was nothing compared to the locals flogging stuff on the beach. First we were sold a place to sit, then a fella tried to sell us a massage, then a woman tried to sell us a beach towel. "NAME THE PRICE, NAME THE PRICE", she kept shouting. After I'd got rid of her, a bloke tried to get us to buy some home-made suntan lotion. We had to buy a necklace off another bloke just to make him leave. He seemed really happy, so I think we'd paid well over the odds.

It wasn't long before I needed the toilet, but as soon as I got up the locals tried to predict what I wanted. They were all shouting at me – "Cold drinks over here!" "Ice lollies! I have ice lollies!"

"I'm going for a shit", I shouted. The whole beach heard. I'm surprised someone didn't say "I HAVE TOILET ROLLS, NAME THE PRICE, NAME THE PRICE."

TAXi IN TUNISIA

DONKEY TOUR TRIP

Brussels

SUZANNE WON THIS TRIP in a raffle. It was the first direct train from Manchester to Brussels with Eurostar. I say direct but it wasn't. It was a train to London Waterloo, where we had to wait for 30 minutes and then change onto a Eurostar train. Hardly direct. I wasn't in a good mood cos we had to get up really early to get the first train from Manchester Piccadilly.

I used to be brilliant at getting up early when I was younger. I used to start me paper round at 4:30 a.m. so that I'd be back home for 6 a.m. to watch *The Pink Panther* on TV-am, and I never found it tough getting up. Me boss lived above the shop, and I used to have to wake him up cos I'd be there before he was awake. I told him I had to get the job done early cos *The Pink Panther* was on at six. He'd say can't you watch it BEFORE you do your paper round, but I didn't like the idea of that. I wanted to watch it knowing that me day's work was done. I could enjoy it more. I used to love that job.

I used to nick a few chocolate bars, magazines, magic markers, drawing books and calculators from the shop. One day, I was slipping a Mars Bar up me sleeve and a fella saw me. He wandered over. I thought I was done for. He said, "Oi, I saw that, but you're lucky – I won't grass you up cos I've just nicked this lot." He opened his jacket to reveal a few magazines and a small bottle of coke that he'd nabbed. "Be more careful", he said, and off he went.

I got away with it that time but on another occasion I got in from playing out and me mam said, "I've just had a call from Ian's mam and she said she wants me to go round for a chat. So why do you think she wants to see me? What you been up to?" Ian was a mate who I used to flog some of the nicked stuff with. I thought I'd best own up. I told me mam that I'd been selling calculators and chocolate that I'd robbed. She told me off and went round that night to have a word with Ian's mam. Turned out it was nothing about the robbing, she just wanted to borrow £20 cos she was short of cash. Shame Ian didn't flog her one of the calculators so she could sort her budget out. I hadn't needed to own up after all.

Anyway, we were up early getting the first train to London Waterloo. We didn't have time for any proper breakfast so I ate six Cadbury's chocolate rolls instead. They gave me a headache.

There were other people on the train who'd won the trip to Brussels. A bloke came over and said that there was a meal laid on for all the winners at a restaurant in central Brussels that night, and that we should collect a voucher for it from the tourist desk once we arrived at the station. I didn't like the sound of this. I'm not a fan of talking to people for long periods of time when I know I'm never going to see them again. I prefer to be left alone in a quiet corner somewhere, but it's getting more difficult to find places where you can hide in a dark corner. All these new restaurants now have long tables where everyone is crammed in next to each other like that scene from *Oliver Twist*. It's daft cos they cram you in close to each other but then bring all the food you order on loads of different little plates and little boxes so you have to stack your meal. I've eaten off me knee in the past cos there's been no room on the table. I was in one of them Wagamama noodle places and I was so crammed in that someone ate a bit of my chicken on a stick cos they thought it belonged to them.

We didn't meet up with the other raffle winners. We went for a McDonald's instead. I was queuing up, thinking about what I was gonna have, when I noticed an old woman sat in the corner. I'd say she was about 79 years old. She looked in a bad way. If she'd been a dog you'd have had her put down. She had a short skirt on with no knickers – you could see it all. I don't know why she hadn't been kicked out, unless it was cos she worked there and was paid to keep the flies out of the kitchen.

An old person's body is never good to look at. It's sights like that woman in McDonald's that confirm to me that we're living too long. The body isn't meant to last 80 years. You can look after the contents of the body all you want, but the body itself is like those carrier bags you get in supermarkets – they ask you to re-use them but they ain't made to last.

I've seen a few naked old people. I was on a busy train from London to Manchester when Virgin had just brought out those flash new tilting trains with the bigger toilets. I went to the loo and hit the button that opens the electric sliding door, and there was an old woman with her knickers round her ankles.

"I've not finished!" she shouted.

"I didn't know you were in 'ere cos the door wasn't locked!"

As she was yelling at me I hit the button to close the door, but then she gets up and hits the button again cos she didn't realise I'd hit it. The door starts opening again.

"Leave me alone or I'll tell the guard!" she shouts.

"I tried to close it!" I said.

She then falls as the train tilts and grabs the nearest thing, which just happens to be the orange emergency cord that sets an alarm off. There she is with the door opening again like the beginning of *Stars in their Eyes*, a siren going off, whilst falling back with everything on show. I legged it and tried to find another loo.

There are never enough toilets on our trains. Mind you, it's not as bad as in China. I've heard their trains get so packed that some of the passengers have started wearing nappies. I couldn't do that. When I was in hospital with kidney stones, I was attached to a drip. The nurse gave me one of those things to wee in cos she said it would be easier than having to drag the drip on a stand into the loo with me. But I couldn't do it. Me body knows that I shouldn't be having a wee lying down so it doesn't let it happen. It's things like this that confirm to me that I'm not in charge of my body.

We left the McDonald's and went for a wander about. I think it was the rough part of town as there were quite a lot of homeless people knocking about. (I suppose the old woman with no knickers was another sign that it wasn't the best area.) I wasn't used to seeing so many homeless people back then cos Manchester didn't really have that many. I only remember a blind fella who used to sit on Market Street playing panpipes, and some homeless identical twins. Even though they were homeless, the twins still managed to do that thing that twins do, like keeping the same hairstyle and wearing the same jacket and pants. They used to stand at each end of the approach to Piccadilly Station, which I don't think was a good idea cos people would have thought it was the same fella and only given them one lot of spare change. Me dad gets sick of me mam giving their pension money away to the homeless. He was out shopping with her recently and she went up to a man who she thought was selling *The Big Issue* and gave him a pound. Turned out it was just a fella stood waiting for his wife outside Going Places with some holiday brochures in his hand. He still kept the quid though.

I think Brussels has the brainiest homeless people as they asked for change in three different languages, which I thought was pretty impressive. I only know English and a few words of French. I'd just about be able to ask for some chicken (*poulet*) or cheese (*fromage*) if I was homeless in France. I'd get sick of eating the same thing every day.

We wandered about the streets of Brussels for a few hours. The only thing I knew about the place was that the action-film actor Jean-Claude Van Damme was from here. I knew that cos of his nickname – "The Muscles from Brussels".

It's one of those cities that's nice enough but you could do with never seeing. If you've no business being there, there's no reason to bother going as it's like plenty of other places. For the same reason, I've never been to Birmingham – it's probably just like Manchester. Thinking about it, Van Damme could have lived there as he could still have the catchy nickname "Jean Claude Van Damme from Birming-HAM". It's weird how names can make a person. Most really famous people have odd names – Samuel L. Jackson, Clint Eastwood, Arnold Schwarzenegger, Joe Pasquale, Einstein and Stephen Hawking. I think their names helped them. A name gives you respect. Nobody ever shortens Stephen Hawking's name to Steve.

Anyway, we wandered about for a few hours. The guide book said Brussels has the most restaurants in the world, but seeing as we'd already eaten burgers from McDonald's, that was of no interest to us. It's only a good fact if you're hungry.

All that way for a burger. It's not worth going anywhere for one night.

Lake District

THIS WAS ONE OF THE ONLY proper school trips that I went on, and I only went cos it coincided with me mam and dad's trip to Yugoslavia, which meant they didn't have to get anyone round the house to keep an eye on me. They left me brother to look after me once, but I ended up having to sleep in me dad's car due to the fact that all the beds in the house were being used by him and his mates and some women. Me brother's always been like that. After that, they either got me Auntie Nora to come round or I stayed at Joan and Tony's. They were friends of me mam and dad's who lived on the estate. I didn't like staying there cos they had a really angry cat that used to scratch everyone. Right nasty little bugger it was. It was weird cos we got through loads of cats cos our house was on the main road. I'd always find 'em dead in the road on the way to school. Me dad stopped buying them cos he said we were running out of space in the garden to bury them. But Joan and Tony's nasty cat lived for years. I used to sleep on their sofa and be woken up by it sat on top of me. I had to sit there really still until someone in the house got up and persuaded it to move. I was more relaxed sleeping in me dad's car.

Anyway, we went to the Lake District on a double-decker Manchester bus that the school had hired. Problem was, it couldn't take us all the way to where we were staying cos the roads were too small and the bus couldn't fit down them, so we had to walk the last four miles.

Mr Buckley pretended it was all part of the plan. He was the woodwork teacher. He wasn't at the school for much longer after the Lake District trip as he hit some kid on the head with a chunk of wood. It was a rubbish lesson woodwork, cos there was never any wood to make anything with. I don't know where he got the wood that he hit the kid with. I remember one lesson where he gave me a plank of wood and said "Make something." I just varnished it and said it was a shelf. I got a grade B for it. Waste of time that lesson was.

We eventually got to the camp site. Now it was the turn of Mr Morris the PE teacher to be in charge. He was kitted up to the nines in proper camping gear – he looked like someone out of the film *Touching the Void*. He'd made a list of camp rules, one being that we had to keep our area clean as any scraps of food would attract insects. He said if we didn't stick to this, we wouldn't survive the week.

He then made a big error. He announced that people with asthma should stay in the log cabin, while everyone else should grab a tent. Everyone said they had asthma cos no one wanted to stay in a tent (including me). All the teachers had to give up their beds in the cabin so the kids could fit in – apart from Mr Davis, who also claimed to have asthma.

There were only four kids who stayed in a tent. One was a lad nicknamed Pinball after the song "Pinball Wizard", due to the fact that he had one of those built-up shoes that you don't see people wearing any more, apart from Elton John when he played "Pinball Wizard" live on stage. Pinball really did have asthma so he should have had a place in the cabin, but he said he'd find it difficult getting up the muddy hill to the cabin. He seemed happy to stay in a tent, but Mr Morris made a big deal out of it and was saying we could carry him up. I could tell Pinball didn't want to cause any fuss and just wanted to stay in the tent.

That reminds me of a concert I once went to. It was the hip hop group Public Enemy. (I don't know why I went to see them cos they just rapped about political problems that I didn't understand. It was like a musical version of *Newsnight*.) There was a bit of bother in the crowd. To try and control it, some health-and-safety fella came on stage and told us all to sit down. He made this request about five or six times but there were still a few groups of people standing. He went on to say that if everyone didn't sit down, the gig would be cancelled and we'd be sent home. Some more people then sat down, until there was just one lad still standing in the middle of this crowd of about two-and-a-half thousand. "You're gonna ruin it for everyone unless you sit down", he shouted on the mic to the lad that was standing. The bloke on the stage ended up sending a security man to escort the lad out of the venue. I then saw the security man leave the lad standing where he was and make his way back on stage. Some words were exchanged, and then the health-and-safety fella announced, "I understand the man still standing cannot help it as he's got problems with his legs and is on callipers. Let's have a round of applause for him." Like the lad at school with the big shoe, you could tell he just wanted the ground to swallow him up.

Once we had our bags unpacked, Mr Buckley took us all on a walk to find wooden sticks. I thought he was having us collect it to take back for his woodwork class, but it wasn't for that. He said that a walking stick is a good thing to have in the country to help you walk up hills and to beat down nettles and big weeds. He'd brought one with him that he found on another trip here years ago. He'd put loads of these little metal badges on the front of it that showed off all the different places he'd been to with the stick.

We'd been looking for our own sticks for about 20 minutes when Jamie Forbes cut himself really badly on some barbed wire, so Mr Buckley sent him back to base. We got back about two hours later with our sticks and were greeted by Mr Morris. He went ape shit at Mr Buckley for sending Jamie back on his own. He was saying how he knew people who had fainted losing the amount of blood Jamie had lost, and he should have come back to camp with someone. He said they'd had a real problem getting Jamie to a doctor due to there being no phone or car. Turned out that Mr Morris had flagged down a passer-by, who then gave them a lift to some doctor's surgery. He said Jamie won't be coming back to base as the doctor had said it would be best if he was sent home so the cut didn't get infected. Mrs Turner the English teacher agreed that that was the best thing for Jamie and then quickly moved her stuff out of a tent and took Jamie's bed in the cabin.

Everyone was called into the big tent at the bottom of the hill – this was where we went to eat and meet. Mr Morris gave us a few first aid lessons that might be useful during our stay. He went on for ages about how it was as easy as ABC. He said ABC stood for airway, breathing ... and I can't remember what the C was. He then announced that he was going to hire a car that would be there for emergencies. He went off to the nearest town while we sat around rubbing down our sticks. Mr Morris didn't come back that night.

The next day was horrible. It chucked it down non-stop and everything was covered in mud. Everyone crammed into the big tent at the bottom of the hill. We were all bored, so Mr Buckley got us to play that game where you have to eat three cream crackers in under a minute. We did this for about an hour. That's when Mr Morris walked in. He went off on one straightaway. "WHOSE IDEA WAS IT TO PLAY THIS?" he shouted. "WE MUST NOT WASTE FOOD IF WE WANT TO SURVIVE HERE."

Mr Buckley shouted back, "NEVER MIND ALL THAT, WHERE HAVE YOU BEEN?"

It turned out he'd stayed over at a B&B in Kirkby Lonsdale as he'd had a problem finding a car-hire firm and had to get a vehicle brought to him from another town. It was a knackered old transit van. It was just as well he got it though, cos that night Richard who was on the bunk bed above me fell off and broke his arm and had to be rushed to hospital. Apparently everyone was up in the middle of the night due to Richard screaming. I slept through the whole thing. It wasn't until I woke up in the morning and noticed that Mrs Stevens the art teacher had moved out of her tent and into his bed that I realised he'd gone. We were only on day two and already two kids had been sent home.

I wish I could sleep through stuff like that now. I can't remember the last time I slept well – in all the places I've lived there's always been something keeping me awake. People having it away all night always annoys me. There's no need to be making so much noise, and there's no need to drag it out so long. The end result is the same, so just get it done and get to sleep. The problem with where I live now is sea gulls (I don't know what they're doing in London), and if they're not making a racket it's the street cleaner. I don't know how he makes a brush sound so noisy.

After Richard fell out of his bunk, our time in the Lake District was pretty uneventful. Mr Buckley's stick went missing – the rumour was that Mr Morris had hidden it.

If we'd been back in school there's no way we'd have been bothered about a stick going missing, but it just goes to show how dull the place was. I spent the rest of the trip rubbing down the stick that I found. I think that was the last bit of proper woodwork I ever did.

I wish I was better at DIY than I am. A few months back, when Suzanne was away working, I thought I'd have a go at painting the window frames in the flat. I went to the DIY shop to buy all the gear. I get nervous in those sorts of shops as I don't feel like I belong with the rest of the mob who go in them – they are proper men who know what everything in the shop is for, whereas I shouldn't be there. I have the same shifty look that I had when buying cider from Hugh Fayes supermarket when I was 13.

I tried me best to look the part. I popped a pencil behind me ear and grabbed the paint and a brush. At the counter the fella asked me if I'll be requiring a receipt, so I said yeah, thinking that would make him think I'm in the decorating business and need it for me accounts. He got his young assistant to write up the bill while he added up what I had. He said, "Is that brilliant white?"

I said, "Yeah ... it's good stuff."

"No, I mean the shade of it, is it brilliant?" he said.

The game was up. I'd ruined it. He now knew I didn't

have a clue. I was an amateur at this DIY stuff, and both he and his assistant knew it. I then added some rubber gloves to the pile. I hadn't wanted to buy them earlier cos it would have made me look like a bit of a ponce, but as he now thought that anyway, I thought I may as well be a ponce with nice hands.

I went home and started painting the frames and realised I should have got a smaller brush so I could get closer to the glass. I ended up doing all the main bits of the frame with the one big brush, and then I chopped the brush down with a pair of scissors as I couldn't face going back to the shop for a smaller one.

I learnt nothing from the trip in the Lake District. In fact, I learnt a lot less than most of the other lads cos I later found out that Susan Barrick was using her tent to show off inside her knickers for 10p a time. She went back to Manchester with a right load of change.

Me mam and dad had a good time in Yugoslavia though.

A weak end in hospital

I'M INCLUDING A CHAPTER about my time in hospital as it was quite similar to being on holiday. The only bit of my stay in hospital that made it feel different from a holiday was having a tube put up me nob, though you do hear about holidays where you can have stuff like that done.

When I was in the Caribbean there was a hut on the beach that you could nip into and have a colonic. It was run by a little Chinese woman who also hired out windbreakers, which I thought was apt. The Chinese are normally into natural remedies, but there's nowt natural about a colonic. I don't know why anyone would want one. I'm all up for making an effort and having a wash and a shave before me dinner, but a colonic … there's no need to be that clean.

I've been quite lucky when it comes to being ill, which is surprising cos I've knocked around a lot of ill people. When I was at primary school they had something going on where they'd send pupils to go and cheer people up in old people's homes and hospitals. It normally just involved a few of us going to a home or a hospice and handing out a packet of biscuits. I always used to get picked cos I was one of the few kids who didn't bite me nails, so me hands looked pretty decent when handing over a Bourbon or a Malted Milk.

I didn't mind doing it as I used to take a few biscuits for meself, but I did try to get out of it when they added the local mental home to the list. It was depressing in there. It wasn't a place for young kids. The patients had real problems, and there was me, an eight year old, trying to cheer them up with a Jammie Dodger.

There was one fella in there, called John, who was mad but happy. Everyone knew John. He used to get on the number 261 bus into Manchester and sit at the back and get his tackle out. John's nob was the first nob that most girls on the estate ever clapped their eyes on. He used to get it out when we were on our visit. The nurses would say, "John, if you put it away you can have another biscuit." Once he'd eaten the biscuit, he'd get it out again. He'd get through a full pack of Lincoln Shortbreads on his own. Thinking about it, he wasn't that daft. The place isn't there any more so I don't know what happened to John.

I hadn't had a doctor for years, but when I reached 30 Suzanne said I should get one cos I kept moaning that I had headaches and active legs. She told me to get checked out at one of these clinics where they do a thorough body check, which includes someone sticking their finger up your arse to check your prostate is alright. I said, "I can't see that helping me headache." It amazes me that they can now do face transplants and clone people and yet they still use *that* method to check the prostate. Suzanne said I should have me testicles checked for lumps as well seeing as I don't bother looking for them myself. I'm not a doctor – I don't know what I'm looking for. I'm scared that I'd squeeze too hard and end up doing more damage.

The body is weird. It would be good if we could shift a few things about. I've always thought it would be better if the testicles could be put where the earlobes are, cos earlobes don't do anything and the testicles would then be a lot cooler and wouldn't be knocked as easily. For things that are so delicate, the position they are in now is not that great. I'm forever sitting on them. The earlobe area would also be good for checking them for lumps, which you could do easily when on the bus or tube. I would also probably swap the brain and heart round so the brain would be more protected.

I signed up with a doctor that just did the more traditional body check. The doctor said I'm in good shape, which put me in a good mood. I suppose this is why I then signed away me organs. I wasn't expecting to be asked – it caught me out a bit, and I just signed it. It was like when you get stopped by someone in the street asking you to sign up to some charity, and before you know it you're giving away £8 a month to save some panda in China.

I also thought that if I ticked all the boxes, he might look after my bits more carefully so they're in good condition if I die. I say I ticked all the boxes, but I left one unticked. It was the one requesting my eyes. I don't like the idea of having my eyes messed with – they're very delicate. I also don't like the fact that someone else would be using them, as they might be into looking at things that I don't like to see. Plus I don't want to come back as a blind ghost. So I said they can have everything but the eyes.

Anyway, I woke up one day with what seemed like a bit of trapped wind but ended up being the worst pain I've ever had. I was in a right state. I still don't really remember the journey to hospital, apart from the fact that I managed to hail a taxi to take me to A&E. Even though the driver could see I was in a load of pain, he still stopped on the way to fill up at a petrol station and buy some scratchcards, which he gave a quick rub before setting off again. I'm glad he didn't win cos I think he'd have retired on the spot and kicked me out to find another lift.

They were really good at A&E and rushed me through to give me some morphine and ease the pain. Then I was put into one of those big scanners, where they found the problem – I had a few kidney stones. The bloke showed me the images. It's an odd job that the fella on the scanner has. He works on his own, so he probably looks inside people's bodies more than he looks at the outside. Even when he was talking to me he was looking at the image.

Before I knew it, I was in a hospital bed across from a Rasta who had stacks of Jaffa Cakes, a Chinese bloke who was always asleep, and an old fella who had a colostomy bag and broke wind a lot. I don't know if that was something to do with his illness or if he just broke wind a lot even when he wasn't ill.

The doctor came round and told me the different ways in which they can get rid of the stones:

1. Use a vibration tool that doesn't involve cutting the skin

and would smash the stones up.

2. Keyhole surgery. Slight cut to the side of my body and get to them that way.

3. Small Lasers. Go up the penis and destroy the stones.

Easy choice, I thought. "Number one sounds good", I said. "I'll go for number one."

"You can't have that as the stones are too big", he said.

Right, so really I have two options, I thought, one of which I couldn't remember due to the third option of having a tube up the nob being on my mind.

"What was the second one?" I said.

"Keyhole surgery. But we don't like doing that one if there are other options, as there's always a chance of infection when cutting into the skin."

"Tube up the nob it is, then", I said.

"Good. I'll send a woman round to explain how it's done." And off he went.

A woman doctor came round with a few dodgy drawings of how they'd do the operation. I said I wished they didn't have to tell me all the details, but she said it was good to understand what they were going to do as it should put my mind at rest. I don't know which bit of "We'll be using a special telescope, which we insert up the penis, pass through the urethra and into the bladder" was meant to put me at ease.

I didn't have the best night's sleep that night. Mainly due to the thought of what was about to be done to me, but also because my bed was next to the toilet, so the flush kept waking me, and the old fella across the way kept breaking wind loudly, which was then followed with a groan. Then when I did nod off, I was always woken by a nurse who wanted to take my blood pressure or change the drip I was linked up to.

The next day I was wheeled into theatre by a Polish fella. Soon I was part of a big convoy of people being lined up in the waiting area. It was well busy. It was like Asda's car park on a Friday night. A nurse came and checked that the info on the bit of paper was correct and told me not to worry as the doctor does loads of these operations every week. I said, "That doesn't relax me, cos if he does loads of them there's more chance of him becoming a bit complacent. I'd prefer it if there was a bit more pressure – like the operations you hear about where they get together the world's best doctors to separate Siamese twins with the whole of the world's media watching. Maybe leave out the world's media as I don't want me nob on show to all and sundry."

She laughed and a male nurse came along and said, "It's

your time to see the cock doc." I didn't know if he called him this because he only works on nobs or because the nurse didn't like him much and it was an insult.

A needle was shoved into my vein and I was out like a light. I had the best sleep I'd had in ages.

The doctor came round. This is when he broke the bad news to me. He said that the people who control the lasers weren't around today so they'd had to insert a stent instead (see opposite). Which meant I'd have to come back for another operation to have it removed. I'll be honest with you, I felt like calling him a cock doc at that moment.

I don't like having to do things twice at the best of times, never mind when it involves having loads of stuff up me nob. I just wanted to leave it. I'm like me mam when it comes to stuff like this. She broke her arm about two years ago, and the hospital put it in a cast. When they took the cast off it hadn't set right and they said they'd have to break it again and reset it. She didn't bother having it done and now it looks a right mess. It looks like her arm is on backwards. Still, she is now really good at doing trick shots in snooker.

I went back just under a month later and had the stent removed. I'd like to use this opportunity to thank the staff of UCH for looking after me.

University College London Hospitals NHS Trust

URETERIC STENT

Information for Patients

What is a ureteric stent?

A ureteric stent is a narrow plastic tube, curled at each end, which is positioned in the ureter to allow urine to empty from the kidney into the bladder.

Why is it necessary?

There are a number of reasons:

1. It may be necessary if you are having a course of lithotripsy as there is a risk of stone fragments blocking the ureter.
2. To relieve any form of narrowing or obstruction of the ureter.
3. Following damage or surgery to the kidney or ureter.

Where is it?

The stent lies inside the ureter with one end curled in the kidney and the other curled into the bladder to keep it firmly in place. It is very unlikely that it can become dislodged.

STENT WILL BE ON THE RIGHT

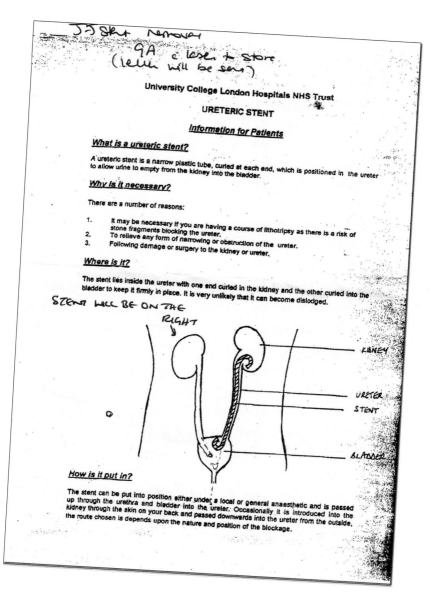

KIDNEY

URETER
STENT

BLADDER

How is it put in?

The stent can be put into position either under a local or general anaesthetic and is passed up through the urethra and bladder into the ureter. Occasionally it is introduced into the kidney through the skin on your back and passed downwards into the ureter from the outside. the route chosen is depends upon the nature and position of the blockage.

MY WARD

Me, a Chinese fella and an old bloke,
Who looked like Mr Burns from *The Simpsons*.
Don't know what was wrong with him,
But breaking wind was the symptoms.
No one visited him or called him,
He seemed quite lost to me.
As well as wind problems,
He had a colostomy.
When I left,
I said "see ya" to the old man.
Turned out the other fella wasn't Chinese,
He was from Japan.
I never found out what was up with him.

THERE WAS A HARD BLOKE WHO WAS IN THE ARMY. HE WAS IN SOME WAR SOMEWHERE IN SOME TROPICAL TYPE PLACE.

HE'D BEEN DOING THE WAR STUFF FULL ON FOR WEEKS SO HIS BOSS GAVE HIM A DAY OFF. HE DECIDED TO GO FOR A WALK IN THE LOCAL WOODS AS HE'D BEEN FIGHTING IN THE AREA FOR WEEKS BUT AIN'T SEEN MUCH OF THE PLACE.

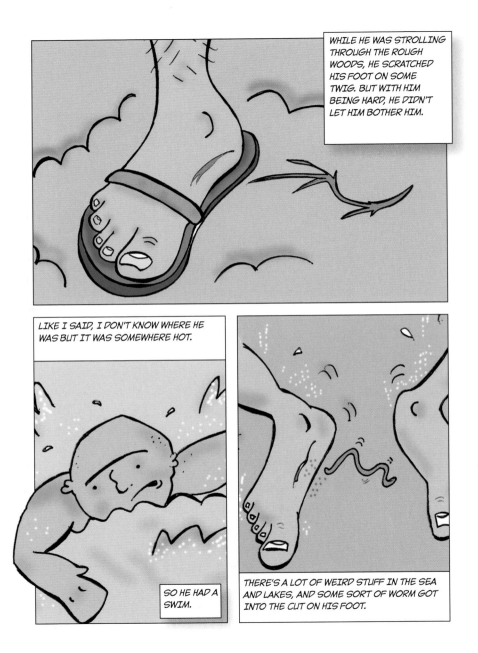

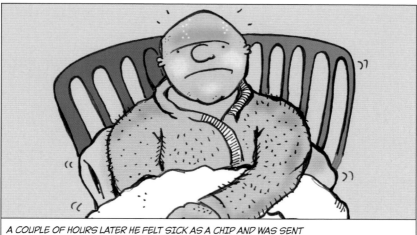

A COUPLE OF HOURS LATER HE FELT SICK AS A CHIP AND WAS SENT TO THE ARMY HOSPITAL. HIS BOSS WAS LIVID COS THERE WAS A LOT OF WAR THAT NEEDED SORTING AND HE WAS OFF SICK.

THE DOCTOR WASN'T SURE WHAT WAS UP WITH HIM AT FIRST, THEN HE SPOTTED THE CUT ON HIS FOOT. HE ASKED IF HE'D BEEN SWIMMING AS THERE IS A WORM THAT CAN GET INTO CUTS AND ENDS UP LIVING INSIDE OF YA.

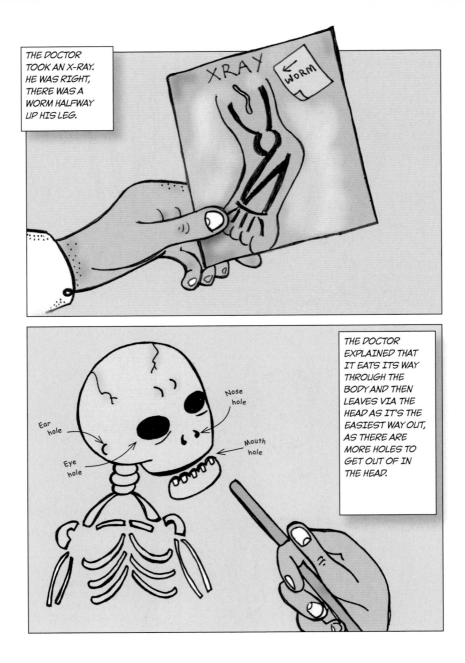

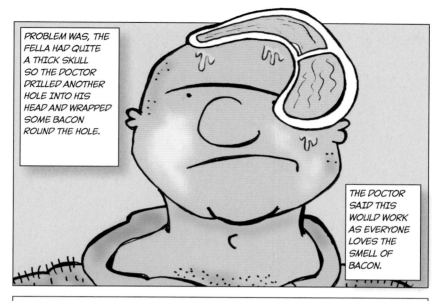

PROBLEM WAS, THE FELLA HAD QUITE A THICK SKULL SO THE DOCTOR DRILLED ANOTHER HOLE INTO HIS HEAD AND WRAPPED SOME BACON ROUND THE HOLE.

THE DOCTOR SAID THIS WOULD WORK AS EVERYONE LOVES THE SMELL OF BACON.

I THINK IT'S WRONG THAT THESE WORMS ARE MAKING PEOPLE ILL BUT ARE BEING TREATED TO BACON.

INSECTS ARE GONNA GET MORE HUMAN COS THEY ARE BEING SPOILT. A WORM SHOULDN'T BE EATING BACON.

Australia

BOX JELLYFISH, crocodiles, snakes (various), blue-ring octopuses, redback spiders, funnel-web spiders, great white sharks. Just some of the reasons that put me off going to Australia. Every creature is bigger and angrier than anywhere else on the world. It's like the place in the film *Jason and the Argonauts* where giant scorpions and other big stuff knocked about.

I put it down to two things:

1. It could be cos spiders, snakes and the like normally hide under rocks. The earth is one big rock. Australia is at the bottom, and they are trying to hide under it. More evidence of this is that you don't get many insects sat on top of a rock. The top of the Earth rock is the north pole. There

are no spiders roaming around the north pole.

2. The only other thing I can blame is the weather. Wherever there is heat, there is danger. I think hot weather makes everyone a bit more violent, even insects. Let's face it, you never hear about Eskimos kicking off – the cold calms them down. The only dangerous thing they've got in Eskimo land is polar bears and look at them – they're dying out cos they can't be arsed fighting to survive, cos it's too cold. Put a polar bear in Australia and within hours the heat would have it in a right mood.

People keep going on about global warming, asking us to turn the heating down cos the ice is melting and polar bears are drowning, but no one cares. They should tell everyone that angry spiders from Australia are moving over here cos of the heat, and then we'd soon turn off one of the bars on the fire. All that stuff about saving energy annoys me. There's Las Vegas with all the lights blaring 24 hours a day, and I have to turn off the standby light on me telly. They're having a laugh.

I don't think I'll ever visit Australia. It's just too far away. It may as well be a made-up place. I wouldn't enjoy my time there cos I would constantly be thinking about and dreading the flight back home. It's the same reason why I'd never climb Everest. It might be a good view, but you've then got to climb all the way down again. People have been up there so often I don't know why they don't just pop down a little path so it's not so much of a pain to get up there.

I look at Australia like Ikea. People always say how good it is, but I can't be bothered going as it's in the middle of nowhere and hard to get to.

Plus the 24 hours trapped on a plane – I think I'd forget how to walk. My legs do that. I once had a really good sleep when I was younger and was woken by the phone ringing in the bathroom. (We used to have a phone in there cos me dad got sick of missing calls when he was on the toilet, and everyone else in the house wasn't very good at taking messages. Me mam still tries to avoid answering the phone to this day.) Anyway, me mam and dad were at work running their butty shop, so I went to answer it. I got out of bed and fell to the floor – the top half of me body was awake but the bottom half wasn't. I had to crawl to the phone and was out of breath by the time I got to it. It was just a bloke who wanted to know if me dad needed any more bread. By the end of the call me legs had woken up.

I never sleep as well as I did when I was younger. I don't really like going to bed cos I'm rubbish at sleeping and the slightest noise wakes me up. I got some earplugs that mould to the insides of your ears and totally block everything out, but then I found I could hear my heartbeat, and I don't like hearing that. It reminds me of the fact that it's me heart that's keeping me alive, and that freaks me out a bit. The other weird thing with these earplugs was the way I could hear my own voice when I spoke. Normally you can't hear your own voice cos you're talking over it, but with the plugs in, my voice was really clear.

I've always wanted to know if deaf people sleep better than anyone else and if blind people stay up later cos their eyes don't get as tired. It's always my eyes that let me know I'm tired. Maybe blind people just get bored and that makes them go to bed.

I've heard that a lot of people go camping in Australia, which I think is mental. If I was to fly all that way I'd want a decent bed, plus I wouldn't be camping in a place where there are killer spiders wandering about. I've only been camping a few times and each time I was glad when it was over. The last time was in Lyme Regis in 2006. I went with a mate who said he had it all sorted. He said he had a tent for me, and his mate knew of a bit of land in some bloke's garden that we could get away with camping on as the bloke was away on holiday.

It took ages to get there cos the traffic was bad. We thought there must have been a bad accident as the traffic was only doing about 10 mph, but it turned out that some local fella was making wooden gnomes on the roadside and everyone was slowing down to look. People love to look at any old crap in this country. We're so easy to please. I once went to a tourist place in Devon that said they had planes and helicopters on show. I paid to get in, only to find that all the plots were empty because all the planes and helicopters had been taken to use in Iraq. People still seemed happy to walk about staring at the empty plots. Mental.

We got to Lyme Regis and me mate's mate told us we couldn't camp in that bloke's garden cos the bloke hadn't gone away, so we ended up camping on the beach. The beach is pretty amazing as there are loads of dinosaur fossils knockin' about. I found a few and then went to set up the tent me mate had brought for me. It was tiny. I had to shove me head in one corner and me feet in another.

Some older people turned up and lit a fire. They offered us sausages, which me mate said is code for swingers, so we ignored them. I didn't sleep much that night as I was worried about the swingers breaking into me tent, and I kept getting woken up by loud bangs from our fire, which was making bits of flint on the beach explode. That's probably why the dinosaurs died out – from exhaustion due to no sleep, due to the noise of flints going off in the cavemen's fires. Maybe.

The only thing that I would like to go to Australia to see is the whales. Me and Suzanne once went on a boat trip in Corfu that promised "a journey to the ocean's twilight zone". We were told we might see some small whales on the trip, but we didn't. All we saw was a turtle's head, and I didn't really get to see that as Suzanne was being sick at the time cos we'd been out at sea for ages. The fella on the boat said this was good as the turtles think it's food. This made Suzanne be sick some more.

On nature programmes they always say the noise from a whale is amazing. It isn't. Once I went to a place in London to get a posh face wash that a mate got me for free – as I always get spots due to eating a lot of Twix and Madeira cake I thought I'd give it a go. I lay down in this dark room with me head on a comfy cushion and a woman gently rubbing some cleaning stuff in me face, which was all very nice. Then some whale noises came on the CD player. It was doing me head in. I asked her to turn it off.

"It's relaxing", she said.

"It isn't", I said. "It's just noise. And how do you know it's relaxing? We don't know what the whale is saying. It might be moaning about stuff. It sounds like it's moaning."

She swapped it for a panpipes CD.

I don't know why people don't just like peace and quiet. London is a really stressful place as it is, without adding some noise from a mammal that isn't meant to be round here. There was a whale in the Thames a couple of years ago, it only lasted a day or two before it died from the stress. Like I said, it's stressful in London.

So, back to Australia. I think I'd quite like to meet some proper Aborigines. It amazes me the way these people still live like cavemen did years ago. They waste nothing and have a use for everything. I saw some pictures in the paper about some tribe somewhere who chucked their spears at a helicopter that tried to land near them. If the tribe got annoyed with you, they'd let you know by shaking their nob at you. Again, this proves me point that they get a use out of everything. Maybe this is also where the saying "getting a bollocking" comes from.

I don't know what the women do if they get annoyed.

Saying all that though, I'm not interested enough in them to fly all that way.

Future travel

THERE'S TALK about booking trips into space. The people in charge of the idea say this is amazing as every child who dreamt of going to space can now turn the dream into reality. But when you're a kid you wish for all sorts and then grow out of the idea. I wanted a dinosaur for a pet but have since learnt that it wouldn't have been a good idea.

I should really be happy that tourists will be going to space, as I reckon it'll add value to the 1777 acres of land I own on the Moon (see certificate on next page). I can't see meself ever going there though. Suzanne bought me a cherry tree in Ireland and I ain't been over to see that yet, so if I can't be bothered going to Ireland to see me tree then I'll probably never get round to setting foot on the Moon.

Lunar Map

AREA ___J-8 / Q DELTA___ LOT # ___351___

APPROXIMATE LATITUDE __24º - 28º S.__ LONGITUDE __0º - 4º E.__

Lunar Deed

From the recognized authority of the Lighted Lunar Surface, this document represents the issuing of 10 (ten) sercas on the Lighted Lunar Surface.

This deed is for the Lunar property listed below:

Lunar Description:
Area J-8, Quadrant Delta, Lot Number _351_
This property is located _016_ **squares south and** _021_ **squares east of the extreme northwest corner of the recognized Lunar chart.**

(Ten sercas equals approximately 1,777.58 acres)

This deed is recorded in the Lunar Embassy located in Rio Vista, California, United States of America, and in the name of _KARL PILKINGTON_ from hereinafter known as owner of above mentioned property.
This deed is transferable or tradeable or assignable upon the decision of the owner at his or her discretion.

This document conforms to all of the Lunar Real Estate Regulations set forth by the Head Cheese, (Dennis M. Hope) and shall be considered in proper order when his signature and seal are affixed to this document.

This sale approved by the Board of Realtor.
The Omnipitant Ruler of the Lighted Lunar Surface.

_____   10/26/00
The Head Cheese   Dated

Transfer of Ownership

This is one of 54 (Fifty-Four)
Sovereign Worlds of Hope

TRANSFEREE NAME	DATE
TRANSFEREE NAME	DATE
TRANSFEREE NAME	DATE

"This is a novelty gift."

©Copyright 1980™

TRANSFEREE NAME	DATE

The Sovereign

Established 1980

Worlds of Hope™

Years ago holidays were what you went on to rest, but now, due to people not doing jobs that wear them out, they go on holidays that wear them out instead. Airports used to be full of people with just one suitcase containing a few T-shirts and shorts, whereas now people are carrying golf clubs, surf boards, scuba diving kit and climbing gear. I met a professor last year who was telling me that the reason people do dangerous stuff like climbing and jet skiing is because we like the thrill of danger. It's still in us from ages ago when we were cavemen and had to leg it from dinosaurs and stuff.

I told him I didn't do anything that dangerous. He said, "I bet you do." After about 15 minutes I remembered that I sometimes hang out of one of the windows in the flat when I have to clean them, as two are jammed shut from the frames being painted, so I need to lean right out of the one that does open to clean the others. He said, "There you go then – that's the dangerous thing you do." I didn't agree but I couldn't be bothered arguing about it. I clean them cos I don't like dirty windows, not for the buzz from danger. What's really annoying is, my windows are clean but I can now see that the neighbours' windows across the road are filthy, so I may as well not have bothered cleaning my own.

Space is space at the end of the day. Nothing there but

space, so I don't know what the attraction is. You'd still get people taking their cameras out though and start taking pictures of it.

The other problem with space tourism is that if any Tom, Dick or Harry can go into space for a weekend break, I think this will be the end of people wanting to be astronauts. It won't seem as special anymore. You'd be trying to fix a satellite or something while being hassled by someone who wants to sit on it and have their picture taken.

People seem to want to get further and further away from where they live. I don't know why. Maybe it's cos mobile phones and e-mail have made the world feel smaller. No matter where you go, people can still get hold of you, you can still get English newspapers, and satellite telly means you don't have to miss *Coronation Street*. This has forced us to want to go where no man has been before. Saying that, someone told me that if you go into space and put the telly on, you get old episodes of programmes that were broadcast years ago. It's like UK Gold.

I read in a science magazine that the static you get on your TV when it isn't tuned in properly is the radiation left over from when the big bang happened. I find this hard to believe though, when I can't even pick up Channel 5 without having to switch on the digital Freeview box.

"Only Fools and Horses is on again."
"Oh I like this one. It's the one when Del Boy falls through the bar."

I reckon overcrowding has also made us want to go into space. Six billion people are now on our planet – it was never designed to have that many on it. We'll have to start thinking about living underground to fit us all in. I suppose that has already started, with people living in basement flats.

Even though it's getting really cramped, people go and create new things like pug dogs and labradoodles that we didn't need but have now got clogging up the place. And then we make it worse by moving things from place to place. Like alpacas. I read that alpacas used to be quite happy living on the side of the Alps, but then someone brought a few down to the city, they had baby alpacas, and when people tried to put them back on the Alps they didn't like it. So they ended up staying in the cities, and now they're getting in our way.

The good thing about going to another planet is that we could start afresh and have a clear out of the creatures we don't need. If I had to make a list of creatures to save, an alpaca would not get a look in. I've heard bees are quite important. I was watching *Springwatch* with Bill Oddie recently, and he said the human race would die out within six years if there were no bees, so I'd take some of them. Easy to carry as well.

There's all this talk of moving to Mars as it's got everything we need to survive. The problem is, though, it's smaller than planet Earth, so I don't see the point. Nobody downgrades when they move – you move to get more space. There's no history on Mars either, which would be weird. There'd be no point harping on about Henry the Eighth or World War II cos none of it would be relevant any more. Even *Antiques Roadshow* would die out, cos you wouldn't relate to any of the stuff that Michael Aspel was talking about.

One good thing about Mars is that it has 687 days to a year. On Earth we're running out of days for anniversaries as they've all been taken up with things that happened ages ago – St Patrick's Day, Easter, Christmas, Pancake Day, Children in Need Day, and all that. On Mars we can celebrate more recent stuff with some of the new days. Having more days in the year means people will have to wait longer for their birthday, but it also means that when you buy a new sofa and don't have to pay anything for the first year, you'd have 687 days to save up for it. So there's good and bad things about a move to Mars. Days will be about 30 minutes longer as well. I think they will use this as a selling point to make people move there, cos people are always saying there's not enough hours in a day.

If you want to know what it would be like to live on Mars, the experts suggest you visit a place in California called Death Valley. They say it looks just like it. I've never heard anyone raving about that place, so it can't be that good. Mind you, the name doesn't help. It's like that place in America called Tornado Alley. God knows why people move there. I'm guessing even the *House Doctor* on Channel 5 would have problems selling houses in a place with a name like that. "And the good thing with this location – hang your washing out and it's dry in minutes."

I don't know if we'll ever move to Mars, but if we do, at least people will have a decent reason to be driving 4x4s.

WELL IF YOU GOT TO THIS PAGE IT MUST MEAN
THAT YOU ENJOYED READING IT.... UNLESS YOU'RE
CHINESE AND FORGOT IT WAS AN ENGLISH BOOK.
(THEY READ BOOKS FROM BACK TO FRONT... I THINK)
HOPE YOU ENJOYED IT ANYWAY, AND IT HELPS YOU PICK
YOUR NEXT HOLIDAY DESTINATION.
I AIN'T GOT ANYMORE HOLIDAYS BOOKED AS ME AND SUZANNE
ARE SAVING FOR A BRAND NEW BOILER. CONSIDERING
ALL THEY DO IS HEAT THE WATER, THEY'RE BLOODY
EXPENSIVE.... ALOT MORE THAN A KETTLE THAT DOES THE
SAME BLOODY JOB.

DON'T FORGET YOU CAN LOOK AT KARLPILKINGTON.COM
TO FIND OUT IF I'M DOING ANYMORE BOOKS OR PODCASTS
WITH RICKY OR STEVE.

SEEING AS RICKY GAVE ME A QUOTE FOR THE FRONT OF
THE BOOK I SUPPOSE IT'S ONLY FAIR THAT I GIVE HIS NEW
STAND UP DVD A MENTION. IT'S CALLED 'FAME' AND I'VE
MADE A SHORT FILM THAT'S ON IT ABOUT A FELLA WHO'S
GONNA LIVE FOREVER. HIS NAME'S HOWARD. HE'S A NICE
BLOKE, SO LOOK OUT FOR THAT.

SEE YA.